Improving the Allocation and Execution of Army Facility Sustainment Funding

ELLEN M. PINT, BETH E. LACHMAN, KATHERINE ANANIA, CONNOR P. JACKSON

 ARROYO CENTER

Prepared for the United States Army
Approved for public release; distribution unlimited

For more information on this publication, visit www.rand.org/t/RR3240

Library of Congress Cataloging-in-Publication Data is available for this publication.
ISBN: 978-1-9774-0352-0

Published by the RAND Corporation, Santa Monica, Calif.
© Copyright 2020 RAND Corporation
RAND® is a registered trademark.

Cover: Ridgway Hall, Fort Benning, Georgia
Photo by Beth E. Lachman

Limited Print and Electronic Distribution Rights

This document and trademark(s) contained herein are protected by law. This representation of RAND intellectual property is provided for noncommercial use only. Unauthorized posting of this publication online is prohibited. Permission is given to duplicate this document for personal use only, as long as it is unaltered and complete. Permission is required from RAND to reproduce, or reuse in another form, any of its research documents for commercial use. For information on reprint and linking permissions, please visit www.rand.org/pubs/permissions.

The RAND Corporation is a research organization that develops solutions to public policy challenges to help make communities throughout the world safer and more secure, healthier and more prosperous. RAND is nonprofit, nonpartisan, and committed to the public interest.

RAND's publications do not necessarily reflect the opinions of its research clients and sponsors.

Support RAND
Make a tax-deductible charitable contribution at
www.rand.org/giving/contribute

www.rand.org

Preface

This report documents research and analysis conducted as part of a project entitled IMCOM Installation Facility Sustainment Improvement sponsored by the Commanding General, U.S. Army Installation Management Command (IMCOM). The purpose of this project was to identify strategies to improve the allocation of facility sustainment, restoration, and modernization (SRM) funding to maximize the benefits to installations within the resources allotted.

This research was conducted within RAND Arroyo Center's Forces and Logistics Program. RAND Arroyo Center, part of the RAND Corporation, is a federally funded research and development center (FFRDC) sponsored by the United States Army.

RAND operates under a "Federal-Wide Assurance" (FWA00003425) and complies with the *Code of Federal Regulations for the Protection of Human Subjects Under United States Law* (45 CFR 46), also known as "the Common Rule," as well as with the implementation guidance set forth in DoD Instruction 3216.02. As applicable, this compliance includes reviews and approvals by RAND's Institutional Review Board (the Human Subjects Protection Committee) and by the U.S. Army. The views of sources utilized in this study are solely their own and do not represent the official policy or position of DoD or the U.S. Government.

Contents

Figures

Tables

Summary

In recent years, the U.S. Army has been willing to accept risk in facility sustainment in order to maintain warfighting readiness. In addition, reductions in Army military construction funding have led to an increasing reliance on sustainment, restoration, and modernization (SRM) funding to address the Army's facility requirements. As a result, most Army installations have not been able to devote sufficient resources to preventive maintenance because they are responding to immediate maintenance and repair requirements. However, neglecting preventive maintenance tends to result in higher life-cycle sustainment costs, because it increases the likelihood that facility components will break down or fail prematurely.

To help address these problems, the U.S. Army Installation Management Command (IMCOM) asked the RAND Arroyo Center to identify strategies to improve the allocation and execution of facility sustainment funding to maximize the benefits to installations within available resources. As part of this research, we visited three Army installations and conducted extensive interviews with Directorate of Public Works (DPW) staff and conducted shorter interviews with several additional installations. We also analyzed Installation Status Report (ISR) data for all IMCOM installations. To learn more about facility sustainment policies and practices across the Department of Defense (DoD), we interviewed subject matter experts in the Air Force, Army Corps of Engineers, Marine Corps, Navy, and Office of the Secretary of Defense (OSD). We also conducted a review of some relevant literature on facility sustainment practices in the military services, other public-sector organizations, and the private sector. In addition, we drew on information collected as part of other RAND Arroyo Center analyses of partnerships, utility costs, and excess and underutilized property.

Findings from Installation Interviews

The Army delegates 85–90 percent of sustainment funding to installations, but IMCOM gives smaller installations a higher percentage of the requirements recommended by the facility sustainment model (FSM), which estimates facility sustainment costs for various facility types based on private- and public-sector benchmarks. Army installations follow a variety of processes to allocate facility sustainment funding, although they tend to emphasize similar factors, such as life, health, and safety; mission impacts; prevention of property damage; compliance with laws and regulations; and commanders' priorities. They also face common challenges. Installations have shortages of DPW staff for several reasons, including past public-private competitions for DPW workload, civilian hiring freezes and other cost reduction initiatives, and difficulties hiring qualified staff, particularly in locations that are remote or outside the continental United States. As a result, they must contract out some of the facility sustainment workload, a process that is typically more expensive than using government civilian employees to perform the same work. Greater flexibility to hire DPW staff would allow the installations to accomplish more projects within their existing budgets.

The transition to the General Fund Enterprise Business System (GFEBS) for real property management functions in 2012 has also caused ongoing challenges at Army installations. DPW personnel reported that GFEBS is slow and cumbersome to use, that it is difficult to enter required data and extract usable management reports, and that there is a lack of advanced training and data dictionaries. Difficulties using GFEBS consume scarce DPW staff time and financial resources. Some installations have hired contractors or developed software utilities to assist with data entry or management reports. Problems with GFEBS data entry and additional training requirements may also be hampering efforts to increase the execution of preventive maintenance.

Installation DPW staff also discussed innovative practices that could be shared across installations. These practices include grouping smaller service orders and other sustainment projects in the same locations to reduce travel time and costs; assigning staff members as liaisons with major tenants to better understand their missions and facilities; identifying alternative sources of funding for sustainment projects, such as tenant mission funding; and establishing partnerships with state and local governments to share resources and reduce costs.

Findings from Installation Status Report Data Analysis

Installation DPW staff generally agreed that ISR ratings reflect the current condition of facilities and can be used to identify specific problem areas. However, ISR data are not well suited to examining long-term trends because rating procedures have changed over time, and ratings tend to be cosmetic, because it is difficult to visually inspect some building components, such as roofs, foundations, plumbing, and wiring. The Army is currently in the process of replacing the facility condition ratings in ISR with those in BUILDER, which requires more thorough inspections by facility maintenance experts. However, it will take time to fund the initial condition assessments required by BUILDER, so the Army will need to determine how to integrate information from ISR and BUILDER during the transition process.

Findings from Other Services

Since 2007, OSD has recommended that the services set their facility SRM budgets at 90 percent or more of the requirements recommended by the FSM. However, since the Budget Control Act of 2011 and sequestration, SRM funding fell to 75 percent or lower and has recovered to about 80 percent as of the services' 2019 budget submissions. In 2013, OSD required the services to standardize their processes for assessing the condition of their facilities using Sustainment Management System software developed by the Army Corps of Engineers, including BUILDER, PAVER, ROOFER, and RAILER. A report by the U.S. Government Accountability Office (2016) found that the Air Force, Marine Corps, and Navy were on track to fully implement BUILDER in 2017, but that the Army lagged behind the other services.

The Air Force, Marine Corps, and Navy follow different processes for allocating facility sustainment funding to installations. The Navy allocates almost all SRM funding to installations but sets centralized priorities. It uses a Condition Based Maintenance (CBM) model to direct 75 percent of planned SRM projects to Targeted Investment Focus Areas, including critical or significant facilities, based on a Mission Dependency Index (MDI) and critical building elements, such as roofs, electrical and mechanical systems, and safety requirements. It also conducts midyear reviews of installation maintenance plans to ensure that they are meeting these targets. The Navy began implementing BUILDER about ten years ago and uses it to predict and plan for repair investment funding over a five-year horizon. It also uses the commercial off-the-shelf software Maximo to generate facility maintenance work orders.

The Marine Corps delegates about 55 percent of the funding recommended by the FSM to installations. Funding for sustainment projects costing more than $300,000 is managed centrally, but the Marine Corps is considering delegating more of this funding to the regional level to reduce administrative burdens. Although they were familiar with the Navy's CBM model, managers said they preferred to allow installations to determine which projects were the most critical to fund. The Marine Corps has implemented BUILDER and centrally funds a contractor team to perform facility condition assessments so that the data are consistent across installations. Like the Navy, it uses Maximo to generate facility sustainment work orders.

The Air Force Installation and Mission Support Center (AFIMSC) delegates about half of SRM funding to installations for preventive maintenance and minor repairs, and the remainder is allocated to projects using a centralized process. The Air Force uses the Air Force Comprehensive Asset Management Plan model to develop a four-year Integrated Priority List of projects across installations. It is based on a probability of failure derived from BUILDER, PAVER, and other systems, and a consequence of failure based on an MDI and Major Command mission impact ratings. AFIMSC is also developing a more centralized process to develop installation sustainment plans using condition assessments from BUILDER and PAVER. In addition, it is using category management to standardize service contracts, such as roofing replacement and repair and elevator maintenance, and to obtain economies of scale.

Findings from Facility Management Trends, Practices, and Research

In the private sector, facility sustainment is integrated with other facility management functions, such as facility planning; engineering and design of new facilities, modifications to facilities, and repair projects; construction of facilities and installation of equipment; and evaluation of facility or equipment replacement projects that are intended to save maintenance or utility costs. The overall goal is to minimize the life-cycle costs of construction, operations and maintenance, and eventual disposal or replacement of facilities.

Public- and private-sector organizations are increasingly linking facility quality and condition with their organizational mission and measuring the effects of facility quality and design on employee productivity, absenteeism, and turnover. They use a variety of performance metrics to evaluate facilities over time and to make comparisons across similar types of buildings. The most useful metrics are those that link financial and nonfinancial aspects, are quantifiable and measurable, and are applicable to a wide range of facilities or projects.

Recommendations

Based on our research, we have identified several steps that could be taken to improve the allocation and execution of SRM funding at the Army, IMCOM, and individual installation levels. We also distinguish between actions that could be taken in the short term and those that would take additional time to implement.

Army Level

In the short term,

- Allow installations more flexibility on DPW staffing within existing budgets to perform facility sustainment at lower costs
- Increase Army-level command emphasis to ensure that unit leadership at the company through brigade levels identifies and pursues corrective actions for non-fair-wear-and-tear damages caused by negligence or accidents, particularly in barracks and motor pools.

In the longer term,

- Improve or supplement the real property and facility sustainment functions in GFEBS, with input from IMCOM and the other landholding commands, the Office of the Assistant Secretary of the Army for Financial Management and Comptroller, installation-level users, the GFEBS contractor, and other stakeholders. Actions could include
  - creating better training, documentation, and data dictionaries for users
  - improving system and network capacity to speed up system performance
  - developing better interfaces to enter and extract data and create management reports
  - allowing cross-communication with BUILDER to update condition assessments and GFEBS's project planning module.

Installation Management Command Level

In the short term,

- Create more opportunities for installation DPW staff to network and share information about common challenges and best practices, including staff visits to other installations, regional conferences, and monthly conference calls on topics of interest
- Develop policy guidance to help installations identify alternative sources of funding for SRM projects, including tenant mission funding and partnerships with state and local governments
- Continue to fund the implementation of BUILDER and determine how to integrate facility condition ratings from BUILDER into ISR.

In the longer term,

- Once BUILDER has been fully implemented, use it to develop longer-range models that show the effects of deferred maintenance on life-cycle costs
- Develop an MDI that could be used to prioritize SRM projects and create linkages with installation readiness

- Implement innovative practices from the other services, such as using BUILDER and other analytical approaches to develop long-range facility sustainment plans and consolidate similar projects to obtain economies of scale.

Installation Level

In the short term,

- Implement innovative practices that have been successful at other installations, such as
  - grouping routine maintenance work orders by location to increase efficiency
  - training building tenants or unit representatives to perform minor repair or replacement tasks
  - establishing long-term relationships with major tenants to help identify and prioritize sustainment projects.
- Increase efforts to identify alternative sources of funding for SRM projects, such as tenant mission funding and community partnerships
- Investigate opportunities for active and reserve component engineering units to perform projects as part of their training.

In the longer term,

- Once BUILDER has been implemented, integrate preventive maintenance with updates to BUILDER condition assessments and use BUILDER to develop longer-range repair and replacement plans.

Acknowledgments

We thank our sponsors, Gregory Kuhr and Michael Grizer for their guidance and feedback throughout this project. We also greatly appreciate the assistance of Patrick Caraway, our action officer, who helped with installation visits, obtaining data, and scheduling briefings. In addition, we thank Joseph Birchmeier, Stephen Bonneau, Ismael Melendez, and other Installation Management Command G4 staff members for their advice and feedback on our briefings.

We appreciate the time and information provided by the installation Directorate of Public Works staff we interviewed, as well as subject matter experts in the Air Force, Army Corps of Engineers, Marine Corps, Navy, and the Office of the Secretary of Defense.

We thank Stormy Friday of The Friday Group and our RAND Corporation colleague Kristen Van Abel for their thoughtful reviews, which have improved the quality of this report. In addition, we thank our RAND colleagues Caolionn O'Connell and Bruce Held for their guidance on this research.

Abbreviations

ADA	Americans with Disabilities Act
AFCAMP	Air Force Comprehensive Asset Management Plan
AFCEC	Air Force Civil Engineer Center
AFIMSC	Air Force Installation and Mission Support Center
ARNG	Army National Guard
AWP	Annual Work Plan
CatCode	Category Code
CBM	Condition Based Maintenance
CM	category management
CMMS	Computerized Maintenance Management System
CNIC	Commander, Navy Installations Command
COF	consequence of failure
DART	DPW Analysis and Reporting Tool
DBB	Defense Business Board
DoD	Department of Defense
DPW	Directorate of Public Works
EOC	Emergency Operations Center
EQ	environmental quality
ERDC/CERL	Engineer Research and Development Center–Construction Engineering Research Laboratory
ERV	engineered replacement value
FCG	facility category group
FCI	facility condition index
FSM	facility sustainment model

FY	fiscal year
GAO	U.S. Government Accountability Office
GFEBS	General Fund Enterprise Business System
HVAC	heating, ventilation, and air conditioning
IGSA	intergovernmental support agreement
IMCOM	U.S. Army Installation Management Command
IPL	Integrated Priority List
ISO	International Standards Organization
ISR	Installation Status Report
ISR-I	Installation Status Report for Infrastructure
IT	information technology
MAJCOM	Major Command
MARFORRES	U.S. Marine Corps Forces Reserve
MDI	Mission Dependency Index
MILCON	military construction
MOA	Memorandum of Agreement
MOU	Memorandum of Understanding
MP	Military Police
NTC	National Training Center
ORI	Operational Readiness Index
OSD	Office of the Secretary of Defense
OSHA	Occupational Safety and Health Administration
POF	probability of failure
PW	public works
QS	Quality Score
R&M	restoration and modernization
RAC	Risk Assessment Code
RDT&E	Research, Development, Test, and Evaluation
RMG	Reform Management Group
ROI	return on investment

SCIF	Sensitive Compartmented Information Facility
SMS	Sustainment Management System
SRM	sustainment, restoration, and modernization
TDA	Table of Distribution and Allowances
UPH	Unaccompanied Personnel Housing
USAG	U.S. Army Garrison
USAR	U.S. Army Reserve
VAST	Visible Asset Sustainment Tool

CHAPTER ONE

Introduction

Background and Purpose

Infrastructure challenges are an increasing concern across the U.S. Army, because the Army has been willing to accept risk, in terms of an increasing backlog of deferred maintenance and potential degradation of facilities, by underfunding facility sustainment costs in order to maintain warfighting readiness. The Army defines facility sustainment as maintenance and repair necessary to keep facilities in good working order, including recurring maintenance checks; service calls; emergency repairs; major component repairs; and replacement of roofs, furnaces, and air conditioners. Facility restoration consists of repair and replacement work to fix facilities damaged by previous inadequate sustainment, excessive age, natural disasters, fires, and accidents. Facility modernization alters facilities to implement new or advanced technologies or to accommodate new functions.[1]

Large reductions in the Army's military construction (MILCON) funding, from a peak of $6 billion in fiscal year (FY) 2009 to $600 million in FY 2017,[2] have reduced the rate of facility replacement and led to increased reliance on sustainment, restoration, and modernization (SRM) funding in the Operations and Maintenance, Army budget to support the Army's requirements within existing facilities. The Department of Defense's (DoD) Facilities Sustainment Model (FSM) estimates costs for maintenance activities necessary to keep a typical inventory of facilities in good working order over their expected service lives. Over the past four to five years, the Army has programmed for approximately 75 percent of estimated sustainment costs, and U.S. Army Installation Management Command (IMCOM) has allocated approximately 66 percent of those costs to garrisons.[3] Garrisons are then challenged to sustain their facilities with less than the estimated funding requirement, and responding to emergencies (such as storm damage and fire loss) often leads to further reductions in the funding available for sustainment. Installations are permitted to migrate up to 5 percent of facility sustainment funding to restoration and modernization (R&M) projects without IMCOM headquarters approval. Based on data provided by IMCOM, installations reprogrammed

---

[1] See, for example, U.S. Department of the Army, 2018, p. 204. Facility operating costs, including custodial service, refuse collection, grounds maintenance, and utilities, are budgeted separately as part of Base Operations Support.

[2] This is based on the DoD Construction Programs (C-1) budget exhibits for FY 2007–FY 2019, excluding construction related to Base Realignment and Closure, family housing, and the American Recovery and Reinvestment Act of 2009. See Under Secretary of Defense (Comptroller), 2006–2018a.

[3] The remainder of sustainment funding is centrally allocated to large sustainment projects proposed by installations or used to cover IMCOM headquarters costs.

$47.5 million, or about 2.3 percent of total sustainment funding, to R&M in FY 2018. As a result, most garrisons are not able to achieve the industry benchmark of 30 percent of sustainment funding for preventive maintenance because they are responding to immediate maintenance and repair requirements.[4] Neglecting preventive maintenance generally leads to higher life-cycle sustainment costs, because it increases the likelihood that significant systems, such as heating, ventilation, and air conditioning (HVAC) systems, will break down or fail prematurely.[5]

To help address these problems, IMCOM asked the RAND Corporation Arroyo Center to identify strategies to improve the allocation and execution of facility SRM funding to maximize the benefits to installations within the resources allotted. As part of this research project, we conducted three tasks:

1. **Reviewed the current state of facility maintenance at IMCOM installations.** We examined recent funding and spending patterns for MILCON and facility SRM at installations and their effects on measure of facility quality, such as the Installation Status Report (ISR), focusing on vertical structures and deployment support infrastructure.

2. **Gathered information on best practices for facility sustainment.** We conducted a literature review and interviews with Army garrison and facility managers, other military services and government agencies, and private-sector experts to identify best practices in allocating facility sustainment funding, including innovative approaches to reduce sustainment costs while maintaining quality, and assessed the applicability of these approaches to Army installations.

3. **Developed and assessed recommended guidelines for the best use of limited facility sustainment funding.** Based on tasks 1 and 2, we developed a set of recommendations at the Army, IMCOM, and installation levels to improve the allocation of SRM funding to prevent degradation of facilities and premature failures of major systems.

Research Approach

In coordination with IMCOM, we identified a set of target installations for visits, telephone interviews, and data collection. These installations were selected to cover a range of different sizes, missions, and locations, and to include installations whose Directorate of Public Works (DPW) facility maintenance personnel were government civilian or contractor employees, since contractors may have different management practices and contractual incentives than government employees.[6] Members of the study team visited and conducted extensive interviews with DPW staff at three installations: Fort Detrick, Maryland; Fort Irwin, California;

---

[4] See, for example, Life Cycle Engineering Inc., undated.

[5] See, for example, Koo, 2002; SchoolDude, 2013; and Swanson, 2001. We discuss these findings in more detail in Chapter Five.

[6] From the 1980s through 2008, the Army conducted public-private competitions for installation functions such as DPWs and Directorates of Logistics. As a result, some installation DPWs are staffed by government civilian employees and some by contractor employees with oversight from government civilians.

and Fort Riley, Kansas. We also conducted a telephone interview with DPW personnel at U.S. Army Garrison (USAG) Rheinland-Pfalz, Germany, to help capture unique issues associated with installations located outside the continental United States.

In addition, we conducted more limited interviews with DPW staff at other installations, such as Adelphi Laboratory Center, Maryland; Fort Bragg, North Carolina; Fort Hood, Texas; and Fort Jackson, South Carolina.[7] During these other installation visits we were able to ask some selected questions to help verify and confirm findings from the four installations that were extensively interviewed for this study.

With the assistance of IMCOM personnel, we collected and analyzed detailed Installation Status Report for Infrastructure (ISR-I) data on 19 installations (which include 15 additional target installations):

1. Aberdeen Proving Ground, Maryland
2. Carlisle Barracks, Pennsylvania
3. Fort Belvoir, Virginia
4. Fort Benning, Georgia
5. Fort Bliss, Texas
6. Fort Bragg, North Carolina
7. Fort Carson, Colorado
8. Fort Detrick, Maryland
9. Fort Hood, Texas
10. Fort Irwin, California
11. Fort Knox, Kentucky
12. Fort Leavenworth, Kansas
13. Fort Riley, Kansas
14. Fort Sill, Oklahoma
15. Joint Base Lewis McChord, Washington
16. Natick Soldier Systems Center, Massachusetts
17. Rock Island Arsenal, Illinois
18. USAG Hawaii
19. USAG Rheinland-Pfalz, Germany.

For this group of installations we examined trends in facility quality ratings, mission ratings, and readiness ratings over time, as well as transition rates from quality ratings of Q1 or Q2 (green or amber) to Q3 or Q4 (red or black). In addition, we collected more limited ISR-I data on facility quality ratings for all IMCOM-managed installations to calculate transition rates from Q1/Q2 to Q3/Q4.[8]

We conducted additional interviews and a review of some relevant literature to identify best practices in facility sustainment in the other military services, government organizations, and the private sector. To learn about sustainment policies and practices in the Air Force,

---

[7]   RAND staff were visiting the first three installations as part of other research projects, so facility SRM was not the primary purpose of the visit. In the case of Fort Hood, there was a telephone interview with DPW staff.

[8]   Facilities rated Q1 are considered good, Q2 are adequate, Q3 are poor, and Q4 are failing. ISR-I ratings are discussed in more detail in Chapter Three.

Marine Corps, Navy, and DoD, we interviewed individuals from the Air Force Installation and Mission Support Center (AFIMSC); Marine Corps Installations Command; the Office of the Commander, Navy Installations Command (CNIC); and the Office of the Secretary of Defense (OSD) Real Property Reform Management Group (RMG), as well as subject matter experts on facility sustainment information management systems at the U.S. Army Corps of Engineers' Engineer Research and Development Center–Construction Engineering Research Laboratory (ERDC/CERL), IBM, and RAND.

In addition, we drew on information collected as part of previous and concurrent RAND Arroyo Center studies of Army installations sponsored by the Assistant Chief of Staff for Installation Management,[9] and the Assistant Secretary of the Army for Installations, Energy, and Environment.[10]

Information Technology Systems Involved in Facility Sustainment

Army installations use a variety of information technology (IT) systems to manage and prioritize the facility sustainment process. All installations are required to use the General Fund Enterprise Business System (GFEBS) Real Property module for all real property transactions, as well as the ISR-I for facility status reporting. In addition, Sustainment Management Systems (SMSs) and Computerized Maintenance Management Systems (CMMSs) are in use at many installations to improve the effectiveness of sustainment spending and labor. We provide a brief overview of each of these IT systems since they are discussed throughout the document and it is important to understand their basic purposes.

General Fund Enterprise Business System Real Property

GFEBS is the Army's web-enabled financial, asset, and accounting management system. It was the first enterprise resource planning system to be fully deployed within the Department of the Army. It was chosen because it helps standardize, streamline, and share financial and procurement management capabilities data across the active Army, the Army National Guard (ARNG), and the U.S. Army Reserve (USAR). The Assistant Secretary of the Army for Financial Management and Comptroller manages and oversees the Army's implementation and use of GFEBS.

The Army also uses GFEBS for real property management. GFEBS Real Property is "[t]he Army's database of record for the inventory of real property for Active Army and USAR locations" (Office of the Assistant Chief of Staff for Installation Management, Operations Division, 2017, p. 114). It includes some of the capabilities of the types of CMMSs that are commonly used in the private sector, such as work order generation and tracking and the recording of expenditures by cost collector. However, as we discuss in greater detail below, GFEBS Real Property lacks some of the functionality of IT systems that are specifically designed for facility management.

---

[9] The name of this position has been changed to the Deputy Chief of Staff, G-9 (Installations).

[10] Relevant reports include Lachman, Resetar, Kalra, et al., 2016; Lachman, Hastings, et al., 2019; Lachman, Resetar, and Camm, 2016; and Lachman, Pint, et al., forthcoming.

The Installation Status Report for Infrastructure

The ISR is designed to provide Army leadership with information on the functionality and quality of each installation's permanent and semipermanent real property, environmental programs, and service activities. It is used to support funding decisions for MILCON, SRM, base operations, Army family housing, and stationing actions.

The ISR-I is the central reporting system for facility ratings and cost data for the Army, and it directs facility managers to conduct periodic standardized inspections of facility conditions. The inspection results are then recorded in the ISR-I, which generates a quality rating for each facility based on the ratio of facility improvement costs to the facility's replacement value. These quality ratings and replacement values are used to budget and prioritize SRM spending for each installation, as well as informing SRM funding decisions across the Army.

Sustainment Management Systems

In 2013 the Under Secretary of Defense for Acquisition, Technology and Logistics issued a memorandum that required the military services to implement a consistent set of SMSs to provide a standardized process for facility condition assessments (Under Secretary of Defense for Acquisition, Technology and Logistics, 2013). These systems include BUILDER, PAVER, ROOFER, and RAILER, for assessing the condition of facilities, pavements, roofs, and railroads, respectively. Originally developed by the Army Corps of Engineers, the goals of BUILDER and other SMSs are to track and forecast facility conditions and functionality to optimize maintenance and SRM spending, produce data for higher level infrastructure reporting (Grussing, 2012), and achieve cost savings by "reducing inspection costs and optimizing sustainment, repair, and restoration investments" (Uzarski, Grussing, and Clayton, 2007, p. 72). Each SMS forecasts facility conditions by using periodic inspection data to tune a facility degradation model, then uses these projections to recommend optimal times for performing preventive and restorative maintenance to extend the useful life of the facility. Although OSD has mandated the use of BUILDER in facility sustainment planning, the Army has been slow to implement it in comparison with the other services, because it has not fully funded the detailed inspections of facilities and their components that are required by BUILDER (U.S. Government Accountability Office [GAO], 2016). PAVER, RAILER, and ROOFER are more widely used by Army installations.

Computerized Maintenance Management Systems

CMMSs such as Maximo and TRIRIGA are commercial off-the-shelf systems used to generate and track work orders for facility maintenance. CMMSs are designed to manage maintenance work orders from request to completion; gather and analyze data on building components to increase availability, reliability, and performance and reduce life-cycle ownership costs; and help organizations transition from reactive maintenance to preventive and predictive maintenance (see, for example, IBM Corporation, 2016). The Navy uses Maximo as its CMMS and the Air Force has been implementing TRIRIGA. These systems are used at some Army installations, primarily by DPW contractors, although they may be required to use GFEBS exclusively in the future. These systems generally cannot share data with GFEBS, so DPW contractors who use other CMMSs must also key the data into GFEBS.

The Organization of This Report

In Chapter Two we discuss insights from our installation visits and interviews. Chapter Three shows the results of our ISR data analysis. In Chapter Four we discuss insights from interviews and literature related to facility sustainment in OSD and the other military services, and in Chapter Five we present insights from the broader facility management literature. Chapter Six summarizes our findings and recommendations. In the Appendix we provide additional data on the transition rates from Q1/Q2 to Q3/Q4 at each IMCOM-managed installation.

CHAPTER TWO

Insights from Installation Visits and Interviews

To better understand the facility sustainment budget allocation and execution processes at Army installations and the challenges they face in maintaining facilities on a limited budget, we visited three Army installations: Fort Detrick, Fort Irwin, and Fort Riley. We also conducted a telephone interview with DPW staff at USAG Rheinland-Pfalz, Germany. These installations were selected to represent a variety of different missions, locations, and sizes, in terms of acreage and building square footage. Table 2.1 provides summary information on each of these four installations, and we briefly describe the installations' missions, major tenant organizations, population, and other background information in the subsequent paragraphs. As was mentioned in Chapter One, we also conducted more limited interviews with DPW staff at a few additional installations, including the Adelphi Laboratory Center, Fort Bragg, Fort Hood, and Fort Jackson. These interviews helped to verify the broader relevance of the findings from the four installations that we more extensively interviewed and to elicit additional information about installation best practices.

Fort Detrick's primary missions are advanced biomedical research and development, medical logistics, and long-haul telecommunications for the White House, DoD, and other government agencies. Medical tenants include the U.S. Army Medical Research and Materiel Command, the Naval Medical Logistics Command, the Naval Medical Research Center, and the U.S. Air Force Medical Logistics Division of the Air Force Medical Operations Agency. Fort Detrick also houses the National Interagency Biodefense Campus, a group of federal biomedical research facilities, including the Department of Homeland Security's National Biodefense

Table 2.1
Characteristics of Primary Installations Visited or Interviewed

Installation	Acres	Number of Facilities	Total Square Feet (in millions)	Paved Area (in millions of square yards)	Plant Replacement Value (in billions of dollars)
Fort Detrick	1,410	1,044	5.224	1.479	2.504
Fort Irwin	753,537	2,572	8.999	5.871	7.077
Fort Riley	97,111	4,767	21.853	10.480	7.953
USAG Rheinland-Pfalz	10,302	6,442	26.367	9.223	9.062

SOURCE: Office of the Assistant Chief of Staff for Installation Management, 2017, except for Fort Irwin acreage, which is based on U.S. Army, Fort Irwin, 2017.

Analysis and Countermeasures Center, the National Institutes of Health's National Institute of Allergy and Infectious Diseases Integrated Research Facility, and the U.S. Army Medical Research Institute of Infectious Diseases. Fort Detrick supports a total workforce of more than 11,000 service members, government civilians, and contractor employees (U.S. Army, Fort Detrick, undated). Its DPW staff is composed of government civilian employees.

Fort Irwin is the home of the National Training Center (NTC), whose mission is to train brigade combat teams to a demanding standard using realistic scenarios. Tenant units include the Operations Group, which provides observer/controllers and after-action reviews for each brigade combat team rotation; the 11th Armored Cavalry Regiment, which acts as the opposing force to rotational training units; the 916th Support Brigade, which supports command and control of rotational sustainment units and executes rotary wing aviation operations for NTC units; the Reserve Component Operations Plans and Training office, which serves as the training liaison for reserve component units participating in NTC rotations; and the Air Force's 12th Combat Training Squadron, which provides operational control and logistical support for aircraft units participating in NTC exercises (MyBaseGuide, 2015; U.S. Army, Fort Irwin, 2017). Fort Irwin supports a total workforce of about 15,000 military, government civilian, and contractor personnel, including an average of about 6,000 military personnel participating in training exercises. Base operations and routine facility maintenance work orders are performed by contractor employees; larger SRM projects are contracted separately.

Fort Riley hosts the 1st Infantry Division's headquarters and associated units, including two armored brigade combat teams, a combat aviation brigade, a sustainment brigade, and division artillery. Other major tenant organizations include the 97th Military Police Battalion, the 902nd Military Intelligence Group, the Air Force's 10th Air Support Operations Squadron, several ARNG and USAR units, and a Veterans' Administration call center (U.S. Army, Fort Riley, undated a, undated b; MyBaseGuide, 2017). Fort Riley has a population of approximately 28,000 active duty military personnel and civilian employees. Its DPW facility sustainment workforce is composed of government civilian employees.

USAG Rheinland-Pfalz was established in October 2013 with its headquarters in Kaiserslautern, Germany. It was formed from the consolidation of four separate military communities and manages 29 separate sites, including major facilities at Baumholder, the Germersheim and Kaiserslautern Army Depots, the Landstuhl Regional Medical Center, and the Miesau Ammunition Depot. Other major tenants include the 7th Mission Support Command, the 10th Army Air and Missile Defense Command, the 21st Theater Sustainment Command and associated units, and IMCOM Europe. It has a total military and civilian workforce of about 16,000 personnel (USAG Rheinland-Pfalz, undated a, undated b, undated c). Baumholder has a government civilian DPW workforce, but most of the other sites have a contractor workforce performing base operations and routine facility maintenance work orders.

Recent Trends in Sustainment, Restoration, and Modernization Funding

Figure 2.1 shows recent trends in facility SRM funding at each of these installations, based on financial data provided by IMCOM. These installations received 67.6–69.3 percent of the

Figure 2.1
Recent Facility Sustainment, Restoration, and Modernization Funding at Four Installations Visited or Interviewed

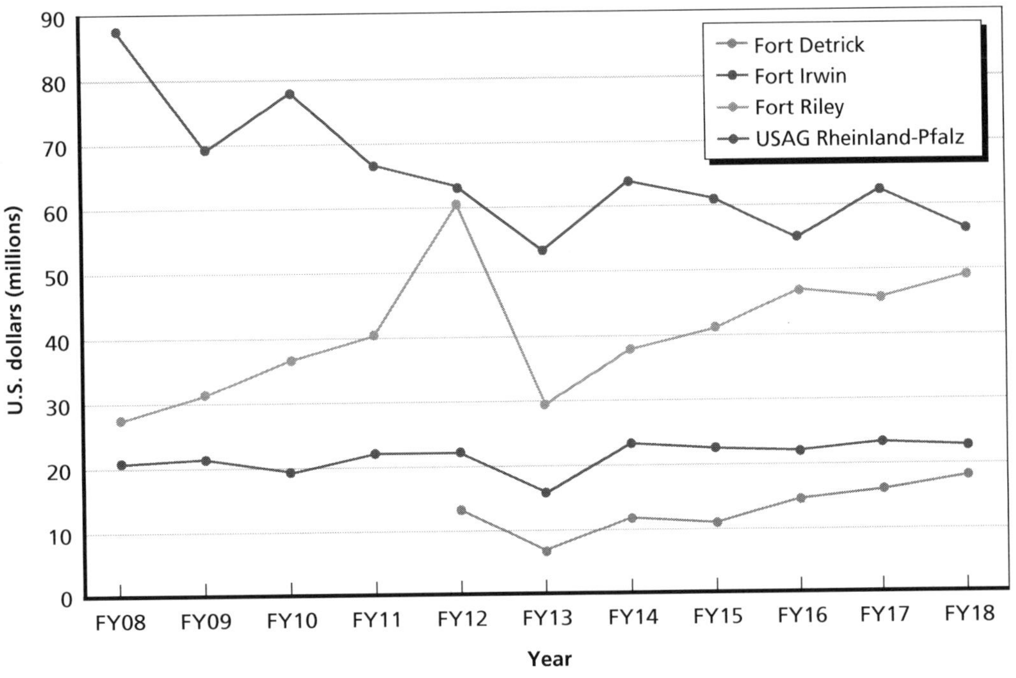

SOURCE: Financial data provided by IMCOM.

SRM funding recommended by DoD's FSM in FY 2017 and 72.0–73.5 percent of the recommended funding in FY 2018.[1] Facility SRM funding dropped by almost 40 percent for IMCOM as a whole in FY 2013 due to sequestration and has gradually recovered since that time. This pattern is reflected in the funding at the individual installations shown in Figure 2.1. Some of the reduction in funding for USAG Rheinland-Pfalz most likely reflects a reduction in Army military and civilian personnel permanently stationed in Germany, from about 37,600 in 2009 to 26,700 in 2018, and associated base closures.[2] Fort Riley received additional funding in FY 2012 for R&M projects.

In the remainder of this chapter we will discuss how each of the four installations we interviewed allocates its facility SRM budget, challenges faced by these installations in making the best use of SRM funding, and best practices that could be shared across other installations. We also bring in some examples from Fort Bragg and other installations.

---

[1] The FSM calculates facility sustainment costs based on facility type, square footage (or other unit of measurement), a location adjustment factor, and expected inflation, based on DoD or commercial benchmarks. It includes regularly scheduled adjustments and inspections, preventive maintenance tasks, emergency response and service calls for minor repairs, and periodic repair or replacement of facility components such as roofs; electrical and HVAC systems; tile and carpeting; and painting. It does not include restoration, modernization, environmental compliance, custodial services, landscaping, waste disposal, or utilities. See DoD, 2018.

[2] The information here is based on publicly available data at Defense Manpower Data Center, undated.

Installation-Level Processes for Allocation of Facility Sustainment, Restoration, and Modernization Funding

Each installation had somewhat different processes for allocating facility SRM funding, although they used similar factors to prioritize larger SRM projects. After setting aside funding for the government civilian or contractor employees who perform routine maintenance work orders and their equipment and supplies, the installations ranked larger SRM projects in their Annual Work Plans (AWPs) based on several factors. These factors usually included the type of facility; impacts on life, health, and safety or the tenant's mission; ISR rating; and the senior mission commander's priorities.

For example, Fort Detrick uses a prioritization matrix originally developed by IMCOM (see Figure 2.2). Projects are scored based on five factors: facility type, work type, justification (including impacts on mission; life, health, and safety; and compliance with laws and regulations), ISR rating of the facility or component, and commander's priority (shown as "Customer Rank" in Figure 2.2). Projects are assigned points for each factor based on the criteria shown in each column, and projects with the highest point totals are funded. For facility type, DPW staff said that they give the highest priority to firefighting and police facilities, child development centers, Child and Youth Services facilities, and barracks, followed by customer service buildings that have a large number of visitors, such as Army Community Services, gyms, and pools. The senior commander designates his or her top ten project choices, but some may not rank high enough given the other rating factors.

Fort Riley DPW staff said that they begin developing their AWP in January for the following fiscal year. Project estimators, who have a long-term relationship with tenants, conduct walk-throughs and ask tenants to recommend projects. Other projects are identified through SMSs such as PAVER, RAILER, and ROOFER or inspection reports for dams, bridges, levees, and the airfield. From February through June, the estimators develop project plans and cost estimates and coordinate with other installation offices; for example, if tenants need to be moved during the project. The list of projects is assigned to one of five categories: life, health, and safety; prevention of property damage; mission impact; overdue sustainment; and "nice to have" and ranked within that category.

Fort Riley's AWP starts with the top-line SRM budget and subtracts the costs of prioritized work until all the funding is allocated. Civilian pay, equipment, and supplies for maintenance work orders are funded first, followed by high-priority maintenance contracts (e.g., lightning protection, fire alarms, elevators, generators), inspection, and a 5 percent emergency reserve fund. The remaining funding is allocated to projects based on their ranking, starting with all projects in the life, health, and safety category; followed by all projects in the prevention of property damage category; and so on, until the funding is exhausted. Command emphasis can bring a project to the top of a category, but not into a higher-priority category. The AWP is completed and ready for approval in August.

At Fort Irwin, about half of the SRM budget is allocated to the contractor that performs routine maintenance work orders, and the remainder is spent on sustainment projects. The DPW staff uses a spreadsheet with a large number of factors (listed in Table 2.2) and assigns points to each factor to rank the projects. The AWP is briefed to and approved by the garrison commander, who may move some projects up or down based on the senior mission commander's priorities. The AWP is reviewed on a monthly basis because emergencies can occur that displace other projects. Fort Irwin DPW staff said that they have a large backlog of about

Figure 2.2
The Fort Detrick Facility Sustainment, Restoration, and Modernization Prioritization Matrix

Factor #1		Factor #2		Factor #3		Factor #4		Factor #5	
Facility Type	Pts	Work Type	Pts	Justification	Pts	ISR Rating	Pts	Customer Rank	Pts
Child and Youth Services facilities, Barracks, occupied High-demand facilities High-impact facilities	10	Structure repair Electrical supply distribution equipment Traffic signals/airfield marking Roof repair, damage >$500K Environmental cleanup Asbestos abatement	10	Mission impact, cannot perform restationing and/or transformation RAC: CAT I—catastrophic (hazard may cause death or property loss >$1M) Federal Facility compliance agreements Force protection, compromised ADA compliance HVAC, nonexistent/nonfunctional	10	Black Q4	10	1	10
Primary road Main utility system Primary parking Grounds, erosion (severe)	9	Roof repair, damage <$500K Fire protection/notification HVAC distribution repair Renovation, major	9	RAC: CAT II—critical (severe injury, property damage > $100K) Force protection, upgrade/added requirement Environmental consent orders HVAC, assist indoor air quality/mold inhabitation Redeployment, repairs IAW mission Damage to government/personal property, severe	9			2	9
Access control point Chapel	8	Interior electrical Pavement repair Interior plumbing Duct cleaning, HVAC Security measures (fences, cages, and bars)	8	Mission significantly constrained Environmental notices of violation HVAC, comfort Quality of life; Army family covenant Mildew/mold concern >10 sq. ft.	8			3	8
Warehouse, temperature controlled Administrative, function Medical facilities (non-500 series) Hangar	7	Exterior lighting Exterior electrical Exterior plumbing Repair/renovation for redeployment units (super preventive maintenance, minor renovation) ADA accommodation	7	RAC: CAT III—marginal (minor injury property damage >$10K) OSHA—violation/correction Environmental deadline passed Security, government property Mission impact, moderate Damage to government/personal property, moderate	7	Red Q3	8	4	7
Maintenance support Administrative, support	6	Exterior siding, painting window/door replacement Utility painting Interior painting Miscellaneous interior work	6	Mission performance, reduced Environmental audit deficiency Mildew/mold concern <10 sq. ft. Quality of life; living/recreation	6			5	6
Community, service grounds Education facilities Drainage, stormwater Parking Roads and bridges, secondary	5	Sidewalk, new or repair Other ventilation Drainage/erosion control Equipment, removal/installation Pavement marking/striping	5	RAC: CAT IV—negligible (violation of standard, property loss <$10K) OSHA environmental regulatory deadline Energy efficiency improvements Stormwater management Damage to government/personal property, possible	5	Amber Q2	5	6	5
Warehouse storage (only), supply Community, recreation Barracks, vacant	4	Outdoor athletic fields Indoor courts/bleachers Locks Signs Miscellaneous exterior structure repair Flooring vinyl/carpet/tile	4	Mission impact, minor Security, personal property Erosion control, required to halt runoff	4			7	4
Fencing Miscellaneous exterior structures Relocatables Wash rack Roads and bridges Tertiary	3	Bunker/berm repairs Landscaping/grounds maintenance New construction, structure New construction, roads New construction, pavement	3	Quality of life; work area Improvement Beautification Erosion control, general	3	Green Q1	1	8	3
								9	2
								10	1
Factor total:	0	Factor total:	0	Factor total:	0	Factor total:	0	Factor total:	0

Total for project: 0

SOURCE: Fort Detrick DPW staff.
NOTES: ADA = Americans with Disabilities Act; OSHA = Occupational Safety and Health Administration; RAC = Risk Assessment Code.

$114 million in sustainment projects, so they have to apply to IMCOM for additional funding for R&M projects, or for major projects related to storm damage.

USAG Rheinland-Pfalz had four criteria for prioritizing sustainment projects: life, health, and safety; meeting mission needs for current tenants; meeting mission requirements for future tenants, and non-mission-essential projects. The types of facilities that are given the highest priority are child development centers, brigade and higher headquarters, access control points, and dining facilities.

Challenges in Making the Best Use of Sustainment, Restoration, and Modernization Funding

DPW staff at the installations we visited mentioned challenges with making efficient use of the limited SRM funding that they receive. These challenges include a shortage of DPW staff, difficulties using GFEBS to manage real property inventory and maintenance work orders, and other factors that erode SRM buying power.

Shortage of Directorate of Public Works Staff

One of the challenges reported by DPW staff at the four installations is a shortage of government civilian employees to plan and perform SRM workload. As a result, most of these installations have to hire contractors to assist with some projects, although contracting out is typically more expensive than performing the same work with government employees. Engineering services contracted out to the Army Corps of Engineers are more expensive than using in-house staff, because the corps must set its prices to recover overhead costs in addition to the direct costs of performing the work. The Federal Acquisition Regulation and other acquisition regulations and policies, including small business set-asides, also reduce the efficiency of contracting out. In addition, DPW staff reported that installation contracting offices were understaffed or did

Table 2.2
Fort Irwin Facility Sustainment, Restoration, and Modernization Prioritization Factors

Prioritization Factors	
Life, health, and safety	Facility functionality
Mission impact	Lifecycle of facility/equipment
Quality of life	Unit impact or priority
Compliance with engineering requirements and laws	Other emergencies or maintenance issues
Resources or energy conservation payback	Community interest (Morale, Welfare, and Recreation, Commissary, Post Exchange)
Compliance with environmental requirements	Engineering analysis and feasibility
Facility Reduction Program (negative)	Master planning
ISR rating	Other mandates
Security or force protection	Time on execution list

SOURCE: Based on Fort Irwin DPW staff spreadsheet.

not have sufficient time to compete contracts due to delays in funding caused by continuing resolutions or other fiscal constraints, so were more likely to use set-asides for small or disadvantaged businesses. At one installation, DPW staff said that the installation contracting office was understaffed, and since it reports to Army Contracting Command instead of IMCOM, it could be difficult to obtain contracting services when needed.[3]

The installations face shortages of DPW personnel for several reasons. From the 1980s through 2008, public-private competitions under Office of Management and Budget Circular A-76 were conducted for base operations and facility maintenance services at many Army installations. Circular A-76 requires in-house employees to develop a Most Efficient Organization to compete against contractor bids to perform the same functions. Thus, even in cases where the in-house organization won the A-76 competition, the Table of Distribution and Allowances (TDA) that specifies the number of required civilian positions was reduced.[4]

Second, due to civilian hiring freezes and other cost reduction initiatives, installations have not been authorized to fill all the positions on their TDAs. At one installation, DPW staff said that authorizations for civilian personnel were capped below their TDA, and at another, the DPW is manned at 56 percent of the requirement. As a result, DPW staff said that they had to turn away some reimbursable work for installation tenants due to staffing shortages,[5] and that they were not able to contract out this work due to constraints in their Most Efficient Organization and its legal interpretation. However, some DPW personnel reported that they had greater freedom under their Most Efficient Organization to contract out projects that could not be performed by in-house staff, but that it was typically more expensive than using in-house employees.

Third, some installations face difficulties in filling authorized civilian positions due to remote locations or uncompetitive salaries relative to the local economy. One installation had recently received permission to expand its TDA, but about half of the total positions were vacant because it is difficult to hire civilian employees when the nearest town is 35 miles from the installation cantonment area. At installations outside the U.S., it can be difficult to hire civilian engineers who speak English, because of uncertainty about the downsizing of U.S. forces, and due to low salaries relative to other potential employers. They said that they do not get funding for vacant positions, so it is difficult to hire more contractor employees to perform the same functions. Even in some U.S. locations, Army civilian salaries are low relative to those of other employers. For example, DPW managers at one installation said that they had challenges in finding, hiring, and retaining qualified engineering staff.

An additional constraint faced by a contractor-operated DPW is that all sustainment projects must be contracted out because the DPW contractor only performs routine maintenance work orders, not work on larger projects. The DPW staff can use government purchase cards for small projects costing less than $2,000, but it can be difficult to get contractors to come to the installation for small jobs because of the long travel distance. They had a job order

---

[3] Over time, the Army has reorganized and centralized functions that were previously managed by garrisons, such as contracting offices, Directorates of Logistics, and Directorates of Information Management. Since these functions no longer report to the garrison, they may be less responsive to local needs. See, for example, Little, 2009; and Weitzel, 2011.

[4] See Bolten, Halliday and Keating, 1996; Keating et al., 2006; and Office of Management and Budget, 2003.

[5] Installation tenants who request maintenance and repair work that is considered nonstandard or above common levels of support are required to reimburse the installation DPW.

contract that allowed them to issue task orders instead of competing a separate contract for each project, but it expired the previous year and had not yet been recompeted. Under the job order contract, prices were fixed based on a multiplier of standard costs published by RSMeans to ensure that the work would be priced fairly (see RSMeans Data, undated).

Thus, arbitrary caps on the number of DPW personnel and other hiring difficulties can increase the costs of facility sustainment and reduce the amount of work that can be performed with a limited SRM budget.

Difficulties Using the General Fund Enterprise Business System

GFEBS replaced the Integrated Facilities System when it was fully fielded in 2012 and took over physical and financial accountability of Army real property inventory, which requires the ability to identify, track, account, and manage real property. The DoD Inspector General reviewed the Army's use of GFEBS for real property management in 2013 and found that the Army did not develop necessary real property functionality and fully implement its Acquire-to-Retire business process prior to deploying GFEBS; did not follow the conversion strategy for converting real property data from the legacy system, resulting in inaccurate data being transferred into GFEBS; and did not provide adequate functional training for real property personnel to perform their assigned tasks. At the time, real property staff interviewed at four installations and the USAR Installation Management Directorate stated that they could not generate real property reports out of GFEBS containing the information needed to perform their day-to-day management of real property, including periodic inspections. As a result, some installations hired contractors to assist them with retrieving data from GFEBS (U.S. Department of Defense, Office of the Inspector General, 2013).

Installation DPW staff whom we interviewed said that they continue to struggle with difficulties using GFEBS. The fielding of GFEBS resulted in a loss of functionality relative to the legacy Integrated Facilities System. Most real property data had to be entered or adjusted manually, and DPW staff at Fort Riley reported that they were still not certain whether they were entering the correct building codes to ensure that they receive funding to maintain some buildings through the FSM. GFEBS users described a large number of screens required to enter data on a single building, as well as difficulties being able to extract key data, such as a list of the tenants assigned to a building, or to get usable management reports. In addition, the system can be very slow if there are a large number of users logged in across the Army. Users also stated that there is a lack of advanced training, data dictionaries, and technical manuals that could help them work with GFEBS more efficiently. Some installation staff, including two GFEBS users at Fort Detrick, reported that they had been able to obtain information by networking with GFEBS users at other installations.

GFEBS also generates demand maintenance work orders and records the labor and materials used to perform the work orders. In theory, it can generate preventive maintenance work orders, but this process requires installation DPW staff to enter data on each system, such as age, manufacturer, warranty information, and the recommended preventive maintenance schedule. Fort Detrick DPW staff reported that they had recently received GFEBS preventive maintenance training from an IMCOM team, but had not yet entered the required data into GFEBS. Fort Riley staff have entered equipment data into GFEBS and are beginning to generate preventive maintenance work orders. At Fort Irwin, the DPW contractor has entered equipment data into Maximo to generate preventive maintenance work orders, and close to half of all service orders are related to preventive maintenance. The contractor then manually enters work order data into GFEBS.[6]

Difficulties using GFEBS consume scarce DPW staff time and financial resources. Some installations have hired contractors to help them enter or extract data from GFEBS. One DPW director noted that installations using GFEBS successfully are also using other systems that help them access and update GFEBS data. Fort Riley has developed software utilities to improve data entry for labor and equipment and to manage DPW supplies in GFEBS. IMCOM hired a contractor, Thompson Gray Inc. (2018), to develop the DPW Analysis and Reporting Tool (DART), which integrates data from multiple GFEBS modules and other data sources to generate management reports. Problems with GFEBS data entry may also be hampering efforts to move toward more preventive maintenance and away from reactive, breakdown maintenance.[7]

Other Factors That Erode Buying Power

Installation DPW staff members also discussed other factors that erode SRM buying power. New missions or tenants may be added without resources to maintain their facilities, or there may be a time lag in receiving additional funding. Examples mentioned by DPW staff included Base Realignment and Closure actions, new Logistics Readiness Center maintenance programs or contractors hired by other organizations on the post requiring facilities, and a new responsibility to manage and maintain cemeteries. Deferring preventive maintenance or sustainment projects due to budget constraints can lead to higher costs of breakdown maintenance or the need to replace equipment prematurely. For example, if roads are not repaired when cracks are small, potholes can form and chunks of asphalt can break off, making repairs more expensive. If pipes, boilers, or HVAC systems fail, there may be additional damage to walls, floors, or furniture, as well as installed equipment, such as computers. Installation DPW staff were aware of the need to focus more attention on preventive maintenance to reduce costs in the long run, but shortages of SRM funding caused them to defer maintenance projects that could become costlier in the future. Run-down buildings and equipment failures also hurt staff morale and do not encourage pride of ownership, which can result in tenants not properly caring for their workspaces.

Fort Riley DPW staff said that non-fair-wear-and-tear damages to facilities caused by abuse, carelessness, or accidents can create additional expenses, especially in barracks. The soldier's unit is supposed to conduct a Financial Liability Investigation of Property Loss to determine whether the soldier or the unit should pay for the damage, but since the unit is conducting the investigation, there may be delays in receiving compensation.

---

6 Fort Irwin DPW staff expressed concern that maintenance history data would be lost if the contractor is required to use GFEBS exclusively in the future. IMCOM staff indicated that as DPW contracts are renewed, the Army will no longer pay for contractors to run parallel maintenance management systems. USAG Rheinland-Pfalz personnel said that their DPW contractor uses a different system for maintenance work orders, but the next contract will require the use of GFEBS, which could result in higher costs.

7 Some interviewees expressed the opinion that the Army had not purchased all of the necessary real property modules in GFEBS and that GFEBS real property elements were designed for industries, such as offshore oil drilling, that are very different from Army installations, and therefore GFEBS was not as efficient and effective for military installation needs as compared with other CMMSs. However, we were not able to independently verify the accuracy of these comments.

One challenge that may be unique to Fort Irwin is that its DPW does not have any equipment on its TDA and recently has not been allowed to purchase replacements when equipment fails. Although staff know what equipment they currently have, it is difficult to identify the line item numbers for nonstandard equipment and justify why it is needed. In the meantime, they have to rent equipment at a higher cost. Fort Irwin also has about 75 buildings classified as "temporary" that do not get SRM funding, including the DPW building, library, contracting office, and education center, which have been housed in modular office trailers for many years.

USAG Rheinland-Pfalz personnel thought that the FSM does not fully account for higher building maintenance costs in Germany, because German building and environmental standards are typically higher than in the United States and there is limited competition for the garrison's facility maintenance contract due to the Status of Forces Agreement with Germany. There is also some additional risk from fluctuations in the euro-to-dollar exchange rate. Another challenge is that since unit commanders only stay in their assignments for three to four years, they tend to have a short-term focus, and it is difficult to convince them that more preventive maintenance is needed to reduce life-cycle facility sustainment costs.

Practices to Improve the Use of Sustainment, Restoration, and Modernization Funding

As part of our interviews, we asked installation DPW staff to identify innovative practices to improve the use of SRM funding that could be implemented more broadly across the Army. In this section we illustrate examples from each of the installations, which we categorize as process improvements, prioritization of sustainment projects, and alternative sources of funding.

Process Improvements

Fort Detrick's DPW staff mentioned that they group smaller, routine maintenance work orders with other similar facility sustainment projects to increase efficiency, because it saves on travel time and manpower costs to perform several jobs in the same or nearby locations. For example, noncritical repairs, such as replacing burned-out light bulbs, may be postponed until there are several work orders in the same building.

Fort Irwin has been able to achieve a high percentage of preventive maintenance work orders because the DPW contractor uses Maximo to record equipment maintenance history and generate work orders. It also recently added a direct digital control monitoring system that manages the HVAC systems in 19 buildings. As part of this effort, the contractor added monitoring points to each system. Fort Riley DPW has been proactive in trying to make the best use of the DPW Analysis and Reporting Tool and GFEBS and DART, including developing software utilities to enter labor hours and parts data and manage maintenance supplies in GFEBS.

Fort Irwin sent a DPW staff member to Fort Hood to observe and learn from facility management practices at a larger installation, and this helped Fort Irwin improve its own processes. In particular, Fort Irwin personnel were interested in learning about how to better organize their Business Operation and Integration Division to receive and process work orders, conduct inspections, develop budgets and annual work plans, and make better use of IT systems. DPW staff at other installations also expressed interest in sharing best practices and lessons learned across installations at events such as workshops and regional conferences.

The Fort Riley DPW has a self-help repair and upkeep program that trains unit representatives to perform minor repair and replacement tasks that do not require a technician. Because they manage a wide range of sites in Germany, DPW staff at USAG Rheinland-Pfalz have a program to train facility managers and DPW liaison officers in units to do ISR inspections on their buildings.

Prioritization of Sustainment Projects

At Fort Riley, senior maintenance workers are appointed as "estimators" who establish long-term relationships with major tenants and their facilities so that they understand their missions and any problems with their facilities. Based on this knowledge, they are able to identify and develop projects for the AWP, estimate the costs of these projects, and staff them through other installation offices to make sure that the project is feasible.

Fort Detrick DPW staff said that if they have facility sustainment or restoration projects that are too large or expensive to undertake at one time, they sometimes break them into multiple phases of several smaller projects over time, which are easier to accommodate in the SRM budget. For example, they mentioned that some water and sewer pipeline replacement projects were broken up into smaller projects over several years so that they could allocate funding incrementally.

Fort Bragg DPW staff said that they would like to use a comprehensive roofing assessment management approach that has been implemented by the Department of Energy's National Nuclear Security Administration and the U.S. Postal Service to replace aging and declining roofs in a sustainable and centralized scientific-based asset management program.[8]

Alternative Sources of Funding

Installation DPW staff mentioned a variety of approaches to obtaining additional funding or assistance with sustainment projects. One important approach is to acquire funding for an SRM project from the Army organization that directly benefits from the project. We illustrate with examples from Fort Detrick and Fort Hood. Fort Detrick DPW staff have obtained funding from other Army organizations to help pay for SRM projects when the facility was important for the organization's mission. For instance, they were able to acquire funding from an Army tenant organization to renovate some installation water facilities in recent years because water is important to this organization's activities at Fort Detrick. At Fort Hood about $8 million of Army mission funds were used to help renovate one of its two Tactical Vehicle Wash Facilities. Since the facility was old and degraded, not repairing it could have potentially caused environmental problems and other effects. (Interview with Fort Hood DPW personnel, May 3, 2019; Smith, 2018). Other installations have also sought Army mission funding for installation water and energy system investments, including SRM projects, when the mission benefits from those systems, especially for energy and water resiliency and security investments. Personnel at Adelphi Laboratory Center said they were considering pursuing funding from one of the research labs to install a microgrid that would improve the lab's mission energy resiliency and security.[9]

---

8 See Wendl, 2018. The National Nuclear Security Administration has saved $111 million since 2003 and the U.S. Postal Service has saved $83 million since 2010 by expanding the life span of roofs and reducing energy costs and water damage from leaks.

9 Lachman, Pint, et al., forthcoming.

USAG Rheinland-Pfalz has also been successful in leveraging alternative sources of funding for projects that they have not been able to execute with normal SRM funding. For example, they used European Deterrence Initiative funding to pay for several projects costing a total of $15 million. Second, Fort Bragg is implementing partnership approaches to reduce sustainment costs. For example, DPW staff at Fort Bragg are in the process of implementing an intergovernmental support agreement (IGSA) with the North Carolina Department of Transportation to provide road maintenance to the installation at a lower cost than with the current contractor.[10]

Other Army installations that were interviewed or studied in other RAND research have also used partnerships to reduce the costs of facility sustainment. These installation partnerships are often with state and local governments and are implemented using a variety of authorities and agreement types, including, but not limited to, an IGSA, a Memorandum of Agreement (MOA), a Memorandum of Understanding (MOU), and an airport joint use agreement. For instance, Fort Huachuca in Arizona saves sustainment costs through a partnership with the nearby city of Sierra Vista for traffic signal maintenance using an MOA[11] and Fort Hood saves SRM costs through its joint use agreement partnership with the city of Killeen, Texas, to share Robert Gray Army Airfield.[12] In some cases, installations have been able to save money by exchanging services and utilizing excess capacity, such as in a former DPW partnership between Fort Bliss and the city of El Paso that was implemented by an MOU in 2000 and was initially a five-year agreement. Through this agreement, the city provided pothole maintenance and some other street maintenance services to Fort Bliss (among other things), while the installation allowed the city to use its heavy-equipment vehicle wash rack to wash the city's heavy-duty vehicles and its tub grinder to dispose of various vegetation.[13] Another way installations can save on sustainment costs is through facility sharing partnerships and land-use deals.[14] For instance, the Minnesota ARNG has partnered with local communities to build and share joint multipurpose Training and Community Centers, and this helps save on facility maintenance and other sustainment costs.[15]

Some installations have leveraged the specialized skills of uniformed personnel to help with sustainment projects, which helps cut costs and can help with Army training. For instance, Fort Irwin has been able to use ARNG and USAR units for some construction projects, such as road and storm channel repairs. Similarly, at Fort Bragg, the 20th Engineer Brigade, a combat engineer brigade assigned to XVIII Airborne Corps, constructed a guardhouse for access control as a training project.

---

[10] An IGSA is a partnership arrangement with a state or local government to provide, receive, or share installation support services. For additional examples, see Lachman, Resetar, and Camm, 2016.

[11] For more details on such partnerships, see Lachman, Resetar, and Camm, 2016.

[12] As part of this partnership, Fort Hood and the city of Killeen share the costs of upgrading, repairing, and maintaining airfield facilities and infrastructure. For example, each year the partners take turns managing and paying for the removal of excess rubber from the airfield, saving roughly half the costs of owning separate airfields. For more examples, see Lachman, Hastings, et al., 2019, Appendix C.

[13] This partnership was operating during the early 2000s and then ended, but it provides an example of an innovative partnership that helped meet the diverse needs of the two partners at the time. For more details, see Lachman, Resetar, and Camm, 2016, p. 116, box 6.1.

[14] For more details, see Lachman, Hastings, et al., 2019.

[15] For more details, see Lachman, Resetar, and Camm, 2016, p. 80, box 4.6.

In other RAND Arroyo Center research, we have also found that some Army installations have been able to leverage funding from state and local governments for energy and water facility and infrastructure investments through partnerships and/or from grants. For instance, Fort Leonard Wood has partnered with the city of Saint Robert, Missouri, for joint water infrastructure. This project was originally estimated to cost nearly $1 million and is being funded with significant help from state and local governments. The state of Missouri is supplying a grant for up to $500,000 for the project, and the city offered to supply the remaining $451,000.[16]

Conclusions

Based on interviews with DPW personnel at selected installations, we found some common practices in the allocation of SRM funding and common challenges in making efficient use of it. Each installation had its own process for developing its AWP, but tended to use similar factors to prioritize projects, such as life, health, and safety; mission impact; ISR or SMS ratings; and commander's priority. Common challenges included shortages of government civilian staff that resulted in increased reliance on contracting, which was typically more expensive; difficulties with entering data and getting useful management reports from GFEBS; and deferred preventive maintenance or sustainment projects due to budget constraints that led to costlier breakdown maintenance or premature equipment replacement.

DPW personnel also provided information about innovative practices at their installations, such as grouping maintenance work orders in the same location to save on travel time and manpower costs; establishing long-term relationships with building tenants; and identifying alternative funding sources for sustainment projects, including mission funding for mission-related SRM projects and partnerships with state and local governments.

---

[16] We should note that at the time of writing this report it was unclear whether or not the Army would accept the city's offer to pay for the rest of this project because of some Army legal interpretations regarding the project. For more details, see Lachman, Pint, et al., forthcoming.

CHAPTER THREE

Insights from Installation Status Report Data Analysis

As part of this study, we examined the extent to which ISR-I data could be used to measure trends in facility conditions over time, and possibly correlate them with changes in SRM funding. The ISR-I is the Army's system for assessing the condition and readiness of facilities and identifying resource requirements to keep facilities in good operating condition and to meet mission needs. Each facility is rated based on specified rating standards for quality and for mission or function. Quality criteria focus on the physical condition of the building (or other type of facility) and its components, while mission criteria measure the suitability of the facility to support the required mission or function. The rater, who is usually a DPW staff member or a facility tenant or operator, determines the color rating (green, amber, red, or black) for each facility component (such as walls, floor, roof, and HVAC system), and the ISR-I combines these ratings to create an overall facility quality rating based on a standardized cost estimate to correct all deficiencies. The facility condition index (FCI), which determines the facility quality rating, is defined by 1 minus the repair cost divided by the engineered replacement value (ERV) of the facility—that is, the quality score would be 90 percent if repair costs are 10 percent of the replacement value of the facility. The mission rating is also calculated by the ISR-I, based on the component color ratings and a mission weight on a scale of 1 to 10 that is assigned to each component, with a higher score indicating that the component is more critical to the mission. The mission rating is expressed as a percentage of the maximum score available if all components were rated green. Definitions of each rating are given in Table 3.1.[1]

The ISR-I also rolls up facility quality and mission ratings for similar types of facilities, based on weighted averages of their repair costs relative to replacement value, to provide more aggregated information by facility type. For example, an installation might have several multipurpose training ranges that fall into the same facility category group (FCG). At higher levels of aggregation, they are part of the subcategory Live Fire Ranges, the category Training Ranges and Areas, and the facility class Operations and Training. At the highest level, there are nine facility classes: Operations and Training; Mobility; Maintenance and Production; Research, Development, Testing, and Evaluation; Supply; Housing and Community; Medical; Administrative; and Utilities and Grounds Improvement. Additional examples of the types of facilities in each class are given in Table A.1 in the Appendix.

The garrison commander assigns a readiness rating for each facility class based on his or her assessment of the installation's ability to meet mission requirements based on local

---

[1] See Grussing, Dilks, and Walters, 2011; Headquarters, U.S. Department of the Army, 2012; and Office of the Assistant Chief of Staff for Installation Management, Operations Division, 2017.

Table 3.1
Definitions of Installation Status Report for Infrastructure Ratings

Rating	Adjective	Quality Definition	Mission Definition	Readiness Definition
Green	Good	Q1 = 1 – (Repair Cost/ERV) ≥90	F1 ≥83.33	R1: Facilities fully support wartime/primary missions of assigned units, organizations and tenants
Amber	Adequate	Q2 = 1 – (Repair Cost/ERV) ≥80 and <90	F2 ≥66.67 and <83.33	R2: Facilities support majority of wartime/primary missions
Red	Poor	Q3 = 1 – (Repair Cost/ERV) ≥60 and <80	F3 ≥50 and <66.67	R3: Facilities present significant challenges to wartime/primary missions
Black	Failing	Q4 = 1 – (Repair Cost/ERV) <60	F4 <50	R4: Facilities present severe challenges to wartime/primary missions

SOURCE: Office of the Assistant Chief of Staff for Installation Management, Operations Division, 2017.

knowledge about the condition of facilities on the installation. The readiness rating can be the same, higher, or lower than the weighted average quality or mission ratings for that facility class based on how well it contributes to or detracts from the ability of assigned units to accomplish their wartime or primary missions. The commander must provide a narrative summary describing the significant issues used to determine the readiness rating for each facility class. For facility classes rated R3 or R4, the commander must also include a list of MILCON and R&M projects that, if funded, would resolve the readiness issue.

With the assistance of IMCOM staff, we obtained detailed ISR-I data for a total of 19 installations, including files for Asset Use Components, Asset Uses, Assets, and Scope Ratings, for FY 2010–FY 2017.[2] We also obtained Assets files for the remaining IMCOM-managed installations to examine the rate at which facilities transition from acceptable quality ratings (green or amber) to poor or failing (red or black). In the remainder of this chapter, we describe our exploratory analysis of ISR-I data using one installation as an example. We then describe our analysis of transition rates between different facility quality ratings.[3]

Examples of Installation Status Report for Infrastructure Data

Prior to each installation visit, we reviewed ISR-I data for that installation to identify trends or problem areas for discussion with DPW staff. In this section we provide examples using data for one installation, which we call Installation A. Figure 3.1 shows the quality ratings for each facility class from FY 2010 to FY 2017. For most facility classes, the weighted average ratings remained between 90 and 100, although the ratings for Medical, Mobility, and Utilities and

---

[2] The Assets file provides the ratings for each individual building or other type of facility. Since some facilities have more than one purpose, each use is rated separately in the Asset Uses file. Ratings for the facility components associated with each use are provided in the Asset Use Components file. The Scope Ratings file provides the rolled-up ratings at the FCG, Subcategory, Category, and Facility Class levels. For analytic purposes, we combined the files into one large database covering FY 2010–FY 2017.

[3] The data were compiled and analyzed using the R language and selected packages. See Dowle and Srinivasan (2018); R Core Team, 2018; RStudio Team, 2016; Walker (2018); and Wickham and Bryan (2018).

Figure 3.1
Installation A Quality Ratings by Facility Class, FY 2010–FY 2017

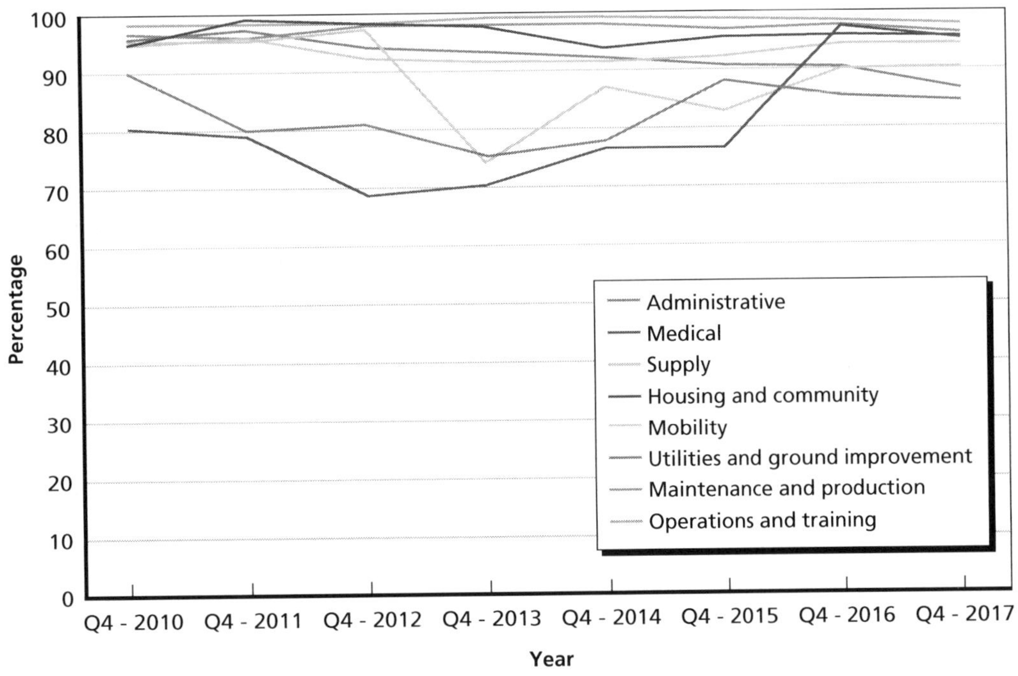

SOURCE: Authors' analysis of ISR-I data.

Grounds Improvement dropped lower in some years. We further examined the Mobility facility class to find which types of facilities were causing the lower average ratings, particularly for FY 2013–FY 2014. Weighted average quality ratings for the subcategories within the Mobility facility class are shown in Figure 3.2. As the figure indicates, the lower ratings were primarily due to a drop in the quality ratings for the subcategory Surfaced Roads. Finally, we drilled down into the FCGs included in the Surfaced Roads subcategory. These quality ratings are shown in Figure 3.3.

Within the Surfaced Roads subcategory, the most problematic FCGs appeared to be Surfaced Roads and Training Area Bridges. Examining the quality ratings for individual assets in these FCGs, we found that some of these fluctuations were related to changes in the number of assets included in each FCG, as well as the ratings of each asset. For example, in FY 2013, there were seven roads in the Surfaced Roads FCG. Five were rated 100, one was rated 62, and one was rated 0. (The latter two roads had both been rated 100 in FY 2012.) The score of 5.71 is a weighted average based on the replacement value of the roads. In FY 2014, two roads rated 100 were taken out of the FCG, and replaced with four other roads rated 100, while the other ratings remained the same. The weighted average increased to 58.67. More roads continued to be added to this FCG in later years, and the quality of the two bad roads was improved to 77 in FY 2016.

We found that Installation A's mission ratings by facility class were generally lower than quality ratings, usually staying in the range of 65 to 75. They also seemed less consistent from year to year, due in part to missing values and changes in the way ratings were rolled up to higher levels. Therefore, we did not try to measure trends in mission ratings over time for other installations. Finally, we found very little variation in readiness ratings from year to year, so

Figure 3.2
Installation A Quality Ratings for Subcategories in the Mobility Facility Class, FY 2010–FY 2017

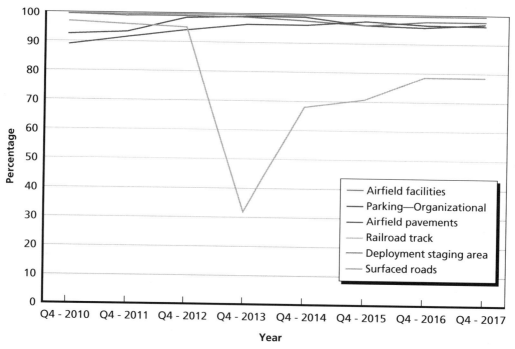

SOURCE: Authors' analysis of ISR-I data.

Figure 3.3
Installation A Quality Ratings for Facility Category Groups in the Surfaced Roads Subcategory, FY 2010–FY 2017

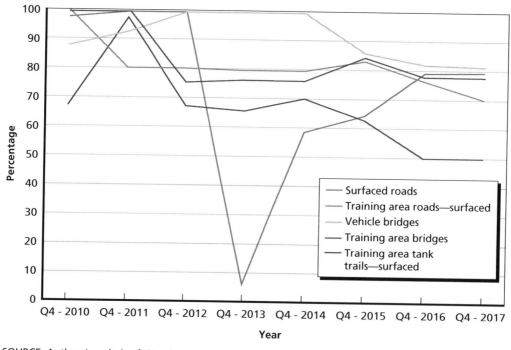

SOURCE: Authors' analysis of ISR-I data.

they do not appear useful for measuring trends. Annual readiness ratings for Installation A by facility class are shown in Figure 3.4.

In addition, we examined FCGs that were rated red or black in the most recent year of data available at the time of our visits (FY 2017) to verify whether installation DPW staff thought they provided an accurate snapshot of problem areas on the installation. We summarize these ratings and list the number and size of facilities with low ratings in Table 3.2.

Installation DPW staff whom we interviewed generally agreed that the ISR provides an accurate snapshot of the condition of facilities across the installation. In some cases, they overwrite the estimated repair costs in the ISR-I to reflect actual repair costs if the latter are higher. For example, Fort Detrick DPW staff members said that the ISR ratings did not reflect some upgrades that would need to be made to their water towers to meet state environmental standards, so they overwrote the repair costs. However, DPW staff noted that one potential shortcoming of ISR quality ratings is that they tend to be mainly cosmetic, because it is difficult to visually inspect components such as roofs, foundations, plumbing, and wiring. The condition of these individual components should be better addressed by BUILDER when it is fully implemented, because more thorough inspections will be conducted by experts in facility maintenance or infrastructure inspection.

Installation DPW staff did not think that ISR data could be used to measure trends in the quality of individual facilities or groups of facilities over time, because some of the rating procedures had changed. For example, ISR ratings were initially done by building managers or tenants, but some installations now have DPW staff do ratings or they provide stricter guidance and better training to building managers to improve the consistency of ratings, both over time and across facilities. In some cases ceilings were applied to quality ratings in some years but not in others based on how certain components were rated. Fort Riley DPW staff cited the example of "4L" standards applied to barracks, which mandated that the asset rating of the entire facility could not be higher than the ratings of the lobby, lounge, latrine, and living area.

Figure 3.4
Installation A Readiness Ratings by Facility Class, FY 2010–FY 2017

Facility Class	2010	2011	2012	2013	2014	2015	2016	2017
Administrative	R2	R2	R2	R2	R2	R2	R2	R2
Housing and community	R3	R3	R2	R2	R2	R2	R2	R2
Maintenance and production	R3	R3	R3	R3	R3	R3	R3	R3
Medical	R4	R4	R3	R3	R3	R3	R3	R3
Mobility	R3	R3	R3	R4	R4	R4	R4	R4
Operations and training	R4	R3	R3	R3	R3	R3	R3	R3
Supply	R3	R3	R3	R3	R3	R3	R3	R3
Utilities and grounds improvement	R3	R3	R3	R4	R4	R4	R4	R4

SOURCE: Authors' analysis of ISR-I data.

Table 3.2
Installation A Facility Category Groups Rated Red or Black in FY 2017

Facility Class/FCG	Quality Rating	Number of Facilities Rated Red or Black
Mobility		
Aircraft loading apron	72.7 (red)	1 facility, 48,083 sq yds (58% of total FCG)
Flight control tower	51.4 (black)	1 facility, 2,000 sq ft (100% of total FCG)
Training area bridges	50.1 (black)	35 bridges, 2,778 sq yds (89% of total FCG)
Training area roads—surfaced	76.7 (red)	1 road, 753,668 sq yds (100% of total FCG)
Training area tank trails—surfaced	78.0 (red)	1 trail, 69,534 sq yds (94% of total FCG)
Operations and Training		
Aviation unit operations	50.6 (black)	2 facilities, 17,198 sq ft (79% of total FCG)
Housing and community		
Army continuing education system center	66.0 (red)	4 facilities, 90,035 sq ft (87% of total FCG)
Dependent schools	53.7 (black)	4 facilities, 185,838 sq ft (33% of total FCG)
Museum	69.4 (red)	3 facilities, 30,574 sq ft (30% of total FCG)
Utilities and grounds improvement		
Electric substations	78.4 (red)	2 facilities, 5,034 kV (16% of total FCG)
Exterior lighting	61.7 (red)	28 facilities, 4,523 units (93% of total FCG)
Power lines	50.8 (black)	6 lines, 1,006,987 ft (98% of total FCG)
Transformers	77.6 (red)	23 facilities, 234,606 kV (98% of total FCG)
Gas transmission lines	51.0 (black)	19 facilities, 458,234 ft (56% of total FCG)
Water lines—nonpotable	49.0 (black)	1 line, 3,470 ft (100% of total FCG)

SOURCE: Authors' analysis of ISR-I data.

Another confounding factor is that some consolidated assets (such as roads) have been split into separate pieces over time, to better reflect the condition of individual sections and highlight attention on areas that needed repair. Thus, we concluded that it would not be productive to try to correlate trends in facility quality with SRM budgets at the installation level due to these data consistency issues.

Facility Transition Rates

One area of management concern at both the installation and IMCOM headquarters levels is the rate at which facilities transition from acceptable ratings (green or amber) to poor or failing ones (red or black). We examined these transition rates at individual installations as well as the overall rates for IMCOM-managed installations as a group. Figure 3.5 shows the average transition rates calculated over the period FY 2010–FY 2017 at Installation A as an example.[4] For each pair of years, the first column shows the percentage of facilities in each rating category in the first year. On average, 80 percent of facilities were rated green, 6 percent were rated amber, 9 percent were rated red, and 5 percent were rated black in each year. The next four columns show what happened the following year to the facilities that started out in each category. For example, reading across the second row of Figure 3.5, 96.1 percent of facilities rated green remained green the following year, 1.6 percent dropped to amber, 1.4 percent dropped to red, and 0.9 percent dropped to black. Red cells indicate that the rating got worse from one year to the next, while green cells indicate that the rating improved. Entries on the diagonal (white cells) remained the same. If we combine facilities that started out green or amber, on average 3.8 percent dropped to red or black each year.[5] Conversely, of the facilities that started out red or black, on average 29.0 percent improved to amber or green the following year.[6]

Figure 3.5
Facility Quality Transition Rates at Installation A, FY 2010–FY 2017

	Q1-Green	Q2-Amber	Q3-Red	Q4-Black
Q1-Green (80%)	96.1	1.6	1.4	0.9
Q2-Amber (6%)	27.8	51.7	14.5	6.0
Q3-Red (9%)	23.5	6.9	61.3	8.3
Q4-Black (5%)	13.9	2.8	16.8	66.5

Initial ISR rating (percentage)

Next year's ISR rating (percentage)

SOURCE: Authors' analysis of ISR-I data.

---

[4]   We calculated average transition rates over several years to reduce the influence of changes in rating policies and procedures. We also exclude facilities rated by business rule, based on their age. Facilities rated by business rule include generic assets (flagpoles, sidewalks, fire hydrants, traffic signals, and signs), assets that cannot be inspected by direct observation (underground tanks and utilities), those with low benefit relative to costs (gates and fences), unimproved assets (unpaved parking areas and roads), and temporary facilities. For more information, see Appendix A of this report; and Office of the Assistant Chief of Staff for Installation Management, Operations Division, 2017, Section 14.

[5]   This is a weighted average based on the number of facilities at Installation A that were rated green (1,146) or amber (104) as of FY 2017.

[6]   Note that these percentages are not directly comparable, since an average of 86 percent of facilities are rated green or amber, but only 14 percent are rated red or black. If we calculate the transition rates relative to the entire population of facilities, an average of 2.9 percent of all facilities transitioned from green or amber to red or black, and 6.8 percent of all facilities transitioned from red or black to green or amber.

Figure 3.6
Facility Quality Transition Rates for All Installation Management
Command–Managed Installations, FY 2010–FY 2017

	Q1-Green	Q2-Amber	Q3-Red	Q4-Black
Q1-Green (70%)	91.4	4.8	2.8	1.0
Q2-Amber (13%)	28.0	54.9	14.3	2.8
Q3-Red (12%)	19.3	11.7	61.0	8.0
Q4-Black (5%)	13.1	5.6	12.9	68.4

Initial ISR rating (percentage)

Next year's ISR rating (percentage)

SOURCE: Authors' analysis of ISR-I data.

Figure 3.6 shows similar calculations for all IMCOM-managed facilities over the period from FY 2010 to FY 2017. On average, about 5.9 percent of facilities on all IMCOM-managed installations that were rated green or amber dropped to red or black the following year. Of the facilities that were rated either red or black, about 27.4 percent of red or black facilities were restored to green or amber the following year.[7] Although these calculations are potentially affected by changes in rating procedures or policies from year to year, they are less affected by the addition of new facilities, since each facility must appear two years in a row for the transition rate to be calculated.

We provide additional information on transition rates by installation in Appendix A.

Conclusions

Based on our analysis of ISR data and our interviews with installation DPW staff, we conclude that facility quality ratings can help identify the facilities on an installation that are most in need of improvement. However, the ratings tend to be cosmetic, particularly if they are conducted by tenants or building managers instead of DPW staff, because it can be difficult to visually inspect some components, such as roofs, foundations, and HVAC systems. The implementation of BUILDER should allow the condition of these components to be more comprehensively assessed because more thorough inspections will be conducted by experts in facility maintenance or infrastructure inspection. It is also difficult to measure trends in the quality of groups of facilities over time using ISR data due to changes in rating procedures and guidance and because some facilities (such as roads) were split into separate sections to better reflect the

---

[7] Note that these percentages are not directly comparable, since an average of 83 percent of facilities are rated green or amber, but only 17 percent are rated red or black. If we calculate the transition rates relative to the entire population of facilities, an average of 5.2 percent of all facilities transitioned from green or amber to red or black, and 5.0 percent of all facilities transitioned from red or black to green or amber.

condition of each section. Using more aggregated data to examine facility transition rates tends to even out some of these fluctuations, but more stable, objective rating criteria are needed to improve data quality.

Ideally, BUILDER condition assessments should be routinely updated after the Army completes initial inspections at each installation and fully implements the system. However, if the ISR-I continues to be used as a source of facility condition ratings, the Army should consider improving inspection procedures and establishing more consistent and objective standards so that ISR ratings can be used to measure trends in facility conditions over time.

CHAPTER FOUR

Insights from the Office of the Secretary of Defense and the Services

In this chapter we examine OSD policies and initiatives related to facility sustainment, as well as facility sustainment practices in the Air Force, Marine Corps, Navy, and Army reserve components based on interviews with subject matter experts and a review of policy documents, reports, and other sources.

Relevant Office of the Secretary of Defense Activities Related to Installation Facility Sustainment

In this section we review some of the OSD policies and initiatives related to facility sustainment, including two policy memorandums issued in 2013 and 2014, the Real Property RMG, and a 2016 Defense Business Board (DBB) study of best practices for real property management.

Office of the Secretary of Defense Policies

The Office of Facilities Investment and Management within the Office of the Assistant Secretary of Defense for Sustainment is responsible for the development of legislative proposals and polices to manage worldwide defense installations, including the acquisition, construction, maintenance, modernization, and disposal of facilities. The Office of Facilities Investment and Management develops budget guidance and establishes funding benchmarks for DoD components' facility sustainment efforts. It chairs the DoD panel responsible for operating and annually updating the FSM, the tool that estimates annual sustainment costs for the DoD's inventory of facilities, which includes all buildings, roads, airfields, ports, training ranges, utilities, and other structures. The FSM aggregates the estimated annual sustainment costs of all DoD facilities to calculate DoD's Annual Sustainment Requirement for the current budget year and the Future Years Defense Program. For any given year, the sustainment metric is expressed as the percentage of the Annual Sustainment Requirement that is funded (Office of the Assistant Secretary of Defense for Sustainment, Facilities Investment and Management, undated).

The Under Secretary of Defense for Acquisition, Technology, and Logistics issued a policy memorandum (2013) that required the military services to standardize the process for assessing the condition of their facilities using the SMS software tools developed by the Army Corps of Engineers, including BUILDER, PAVER, RAILER, and ROOFER. The memorandum also directed the services to record facility condition ratings based on the standardized process in the DoD Real Property Assets Database for each of their facilities by the end of FY 2017.

Similar to ISR condition ratings, these ratings range from 0 to 100 (with 100 being the highest rating) and are based on the ratio of deferred maintenance and repair costs to the facility's plant replacement value.

A second policy memorandum issued by the Under Secretary of Defense for Acquisition, Technology, and Logistics (2014) established three additional requirements. First, the services are required to achieve an inventory-wide standard of at least 80 percent (fair condition) for their facilities' condition beginning in FY 2016. Second, the services are required to develop annual mitigation plans to address facilities rated below 60 percent (failing condition). The plans should provide a recommended action for each facility (such as repair, replace, mothball, or demolish), and estimated cost for that action, and the estimated fiscal year the action will be funded. Third, the memorandum reiterated a goal first established in FY 2007, that the services should submit annual budget requests for facility sustainment at 90 percent or higher of the requirements estimated by the FSM.

In March 2015 the Acting Assistant Secretary of Defense for Energy, Installations, and Environment testified to Congress that 24 percent of all DoD facilities were in poor condition, and another 6.5 percent were in failing condition due to underfunding of facility sustainment, restoration, modernization, and replacement (GAO, 2016, pp. 1–2). As a result, Congress asked the GAO to review DoD's facility sustainment and recapitalization efforts, including progress made in implementing the 2013 and 2014 memorandums. In June 2016 the GAO reported that the Air Force, Marine Corps, and Navy had fielded BUILDER and the other SMSs and expected to meet the FY 2017 goal for full implementation. However, the Army had made more limited progress. It had piloted BUILDER at five installations and requested funding in FY 2017–FY 2021 to field the system at its remaining installations (GAO, 2016).

We examined the services' budget requests for SRM funding relative to estimated requirements from the FSM for FY 2007–FY 2019 based on budget data from the OSD Comptroller's website. These data are shown in Figure 4.1. The Army's SRM budget requests follow a similar pattern to those of the other services. The Army's request was close to or above 90 percent of the FSM requirement through FY 2013, but as a result of the Budget Control Act of 2011 and sequestration that took effect in January 2013, it dipped as low as 62 percent in FY 2015 and has gradually recovered to 80 percent in FY 2019.

Facility recapitalization also occurs when aging facilities are replaced as a result of new construction. The services' MILCON budgets peaked in FY 2009 and FY 2010 and have fallen steeply since then (see Figure 4.2). Solid lines show the MILCON budgets as enacted by Congress, and dashed lines indicate the president's budget request, excluding Base Realignment and Closure, family housing, and funds provided under the American Recovery and Reinvestment Act of 2009. However, the Army's MILCON budget fell below those of the Air Force and Navy in FY 2015 and has remained below them since then.[1] If the Army's facilities are being replaced at a slower rate, this may cause facility sustainment costs to increase as the average age of facilities increases.

---

[1]   As of the end of FY 2016, the Army operated 965 million building square feet, in comparison with the Air Force's 569 million building square feet and the Navy's 471 million building square feet; see DoD, 2016. Thus, the Army's MILCON expenditures should be arguably higher than the other services to replace or modernize aging facilities when they reach the end of their useful lives.

Figure 4.1
Sustainment, Restoration, and Modernization Funding as a Percentage of Facility Sustainment Model Requirements, FY 2007–FY 2019

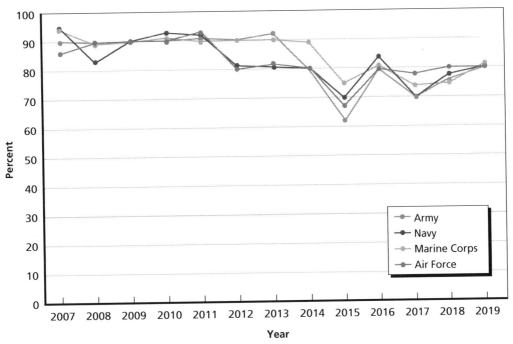

SOURCE: Under Secretary of Defense (Comptroller), 2006–2018b.

Figure 4.2
Military Construction Budgets, FY 2007–FY 2019

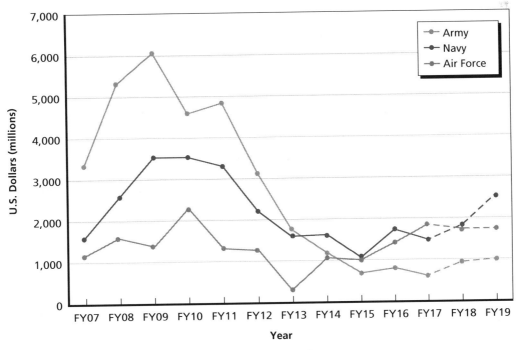

SOURCE: Under Secretary of Defense (Comptroller), 2006–2018a.

Insights from the Office of the Secretary of Defense Real Property Reform Management Group Activities

In 2017, then–Secretary of Defense James Mattis established nine RMGs to implement business process reform in DoD. The RMGs are cross-functional teams whose purpose is "to leverage best practices, centers of excellence, and private sector sources to benchmark and align business operations" (Office of the Undersecretary of Defense [Comptroller], 2018, p. 7-1). One of the reform areas is real property management. The Real Property RMG proposed 15 initiatives, five of which are related to facility sustainment. These initiatives are summarized in Table 4.1.

The Real Property RMG hired PricewaterhouseCoopers as the consultant for Real Property initiatives RP-07 and RP-08. Under RP-07, its original task was to review existing project prioritization methodologies and recommend a standardized process supported by identified best practices that creates effective benchmarking and better articulates resource requirements. Under RP-08, it was to review existing project scoping methodologies and recommend an objective approach to develop and evaluate project scoping efforts to ensure that they meet the true requirement, make efficient use of resources, and identify the most effective way ahead (Office of the Chief Management Officer, 2018). However, based on interviews with OSD personnel in November and December 2018, some of the real property reform initiatives were being revised and the consultant was assisting with that effort instead.

Table 4.1
Real Property Reform Initiatives Related to Facility Sustainment

Initiative	Overall Desired Outcomes	Reform Outcomes
RP-03: Space Management and Utilization	• Enterprise-level Common Operating Picture of facility utilization • Improve use of government-owned facilities by automating the collection of occupancy and utilization data	• Flags hotspots of underutilization and is a critical enabler for possible consolidation, leased space reduction, or MILCON avoidance • Implements business practices and internal controls for data accuracy and sustainment
RP-04: Footprint Consolidation	• Incentivize investments in facility consolidation that drive recurring annual savings and open up available capacity for new missions or leased space tenants	• Aligns the incentives and leadership focus, and resources prudent, service-developed consolidation plans • Services develop and submit prioritized consolidation projects to compete for funding
RP-07: Project Prioritization Criteria	• Standardize project prioritization practices across the enterprise	• Consultant firm will identify existing service processes and gaps and recommend process changes
RP-08: Project Scope Scrub	• Develop a repeatable methodology that ensures a rigorous, objective-based analysis of the functional elements of the project scope and projected expenses against the original requirement	• Consultant firm will identify existing service processes and gaps and recommend process changes
RP-15: Comprehensive Asset Management and Planning	• Identify and advocate best practices for the use of big data and how it can provide decision support for facility life-cycle investments	• Encompasses planning, design, construction, operation and maintenance, sustainment, and disposal phases of the life cycle at the facility component level

SOURCE: Email communication with the Real Property RMG, July 19, 2018.

The Real Property RMG also held discussions with private-sector business executives who manage large, diverse real estate portfolios to better understand their business practices. One difference between the private sector and DoD is that the private sector only distinguishes between capital expenses (which include MILCON and R&M in the DoD context) and operating expenses (base operations and sustainment). The private sector tracks these expenses at the individual building level to manage life-cycle costs. The private sector also has stronger incentives to use space efficiently. In DoD, building tenants do not pay rent, so they have less incentive to consolidate the amount of building space they use. In addition, because the workforce is increasingly mobile, the private sector is implementing more shared workspaces in lieu of a permanent workstation assigned to each employee. Some of the savings from space consolidation can be used to improve workplace amenities. Finally, the private sector is increasingly seeing facilities as part of its human resources strategy to attract and retain high-quality employees.

Defense Business Board Examination Regarding Real Property Management

In 2016 the DBB examined best practices in real property management to identify actions that DoD could take to significantly reduce the cost of managing its real property inventory (see DBB, 2016). The DBB findings and recommendations that are most relevant to Army facility sustainment are summarized in Table 4.2. The DBB found that the private sector has common definitions for corporate-wide data reporting and can combine data across facilities to create an executive dashboard. It conducts full life-cycle costing of all projects and properties and compares them with internal and external performance benchmarks, whereas DoD manages MILCON separately from other sources of funding for SRM, so it is difficult to make trade-offs to minimize life-cycle costs.

The DBB also found that there are few incentives for installation commanders or facility managers to manage their inventory in a cost-effective manner. As missions shift and vacancies emerge, they do not consolidate building occupants and cannot offer contiguous space to incoming tenants, and this increase in incentives for purchases of temporary trailer space or for tenants to move into leased space. Reconfiguring facilities requires resources that are difficult to obtain

Table 4.2
Defense Business Board Findings and Recommendations

Findings	Recommendations
DoD lacks a common approach to data standards, collection, and documentation	Collect and analyze building-level data using common definitions
Senior decisionmakers do not see the fully loaded costs of real property actions	Full life-cycle costing of all projects and properties
Private-sector best practices are seldom followed or shared across OSD and the services	Establish a Real Property Innovation Board to facilitate cost-saving, innovative approaches to real property management
Disincentives and regulations inhibit cost-saving initiatives	Create pilot programs with financial incentives to control costs, such as a tax on tenant organizations that exceed space usage standards
	Establish a real property revolving fund to finance reconfiguration

SOURCE: DBB, 2016.

because any project costing more than $1 million is classified as MILCON.[2] Therefore, the DBB recommended a Real Property Revolving Fund that could make "loans" to cover the costs of reconfiguring facilities. Installations would have to present a business case showing significant savings or return on investment (ROI), and only the best business cases would be approved for funding. Funded projects would be required to repay the loan from the cost savings.

In addition, the DBB recommended pilot projects to create financial incentives for both installations and tenants to control costs, such as requiring tenants to pay rent from their own budgets and installations to use the rental income to pay for building operations. Another possibility is to charge a tax on organizations that exceed standards or fail to meet space reduction targets. In addition, DoD and the services miss opportunities to gain tenants by not sharing facility vacancy information with the General Services Administration. They could also share information with other federal agencies to identify available government space to meet their own needs.

Navy Installation Facility Sustainment Practices

Navy Installations Command includes 11 regions and 71 installations (CNIC, undated b). The Navy allocates almost all SRM funding to the Navy regions for Navy installations, but the CNIC sets priorities. The CNIC uses a small amount of SRM funding to cover headquarters costs. The Navy regions then delegate the remaining sustainment funding to the individual installations. The CNIC requires some directed investments for selected facilities, including 100 percent of required sustainment funding for strategic weapons facilities and the Vice President's residence, 80 percent of the sustainment requirement for shipyards, and 80 percent of the sustainment requirement for the U.S. Naval Academy and Naval War College.

The Navy uses a Condition Based Maintenance (CBM) model to direct 75 percent of planned SRM projects to Targeted Investment Focus Areas, including critical or significant facilities, based on the Mission Dependency Index (MDI); critical building elements (such as roofs, walls, and windows); and essential building elements (such as electrical, mechanical, water, firefighting, and other safety elements). (We explain the CBM process and the Navy's use of the MDI in more detail below.) Installation public works (PW) offices make the facility sustainment allocation with the aforementioned direct investment requirements and CBM model targets.

Navy Risk-Based Targeted Facilities Investment Strategy

The Navy uses a CBM approach to plan and time installation facility maintenance "to reduce the adverse effects of deferred maintenance and repair which lead to accelerated deterioration and restoration costs." Like the Army, the Navy has had facility sustainment investment shortfalls that have caused Navy installations to have "a large inventory of significantly deteriorated facilities and components" (Deputy Chief of Naval Operations for Fleet Readiness and Logistics, 2017). The Navy's CBM process is trying to improve facility SRM while acknowledging that, given scarce resources, the Navy will still need to incur some risks in its facilities. This risk-based targeted facilities investment strategy was started in the fall of 2017.

Specifically, the Navy is increasing emphasis on mission priorities by focusing planned maintenance and repair efforts for all scheduled SRM projects "on the critical/essential com-

---

[2] Since the DBB report was released, this policy has been changed to allow up to $2 million in R&M funding to be spent before MILCON funding is required.

Figure 4.3
The Navy's Condition Based Maintenance Matrix

		Investment Prioritization Matrix								
		Critical			Essential					Low	
		Structures	Roofing	Walls, Windows, and Doors	Electrical	HVAC	Plumbing	Fire Protection	Conveying	Interior Walls, Stairs, and Doors	Interior Finishes
Uniformat II Master		Multiple	B30	B20	D50	D30	D20	D40	D10	C10	C40
Facility criticality (MDI)	Critical (85–100)	1	1	1	2	2	2	2	2	3	3
	Significant (70–84)	1	1	1	2	2	2	2	2	3	3
	Relevant (55–69)	2	2	2	3	3	3	3	3	4	4
	Moderate (40–54)	3	3	3	4	4	4	4	4	5	5
	Low (1–39)	4	4	4	5	5	5	5	5	5	5
		Investment codes (1–5)									

SOURCE: Lynn Ladd, Navy SRM Regional Program Director, Naval Facilities Engineering Command Southeast, February 25, 2019.
NOTE: The "Uniformat II Master" row includes the level 2 group element classification codes from the American Society for Testing and Materials Uniformat II Classification for Building Elements. For more information, see Charette and Marshall, 1999.

ponents of critical/significant facilities, especially where degradation poses the greatest risk to Navy mission, allowing other less-critical facilities to degrade." Navy installation facility maintenance plans are supposed to be developed in alignment with the CBM matrix (see Figure 4.3) to focus investments in the more critical facilities and components. The Navy has directed that "all activities should concentrate at least 75 percent of planned maintenance investments . . . in the 'Targeted Investment Focus Area'" (Deputy Chief of Naval Operations for Fleet Readiness and Logistics, 2017).

Next we explain how the CBM matrix works in practice. "CBM is a Risk Based Investment Strategy to target limited resources for facility investments on the most critical components of the most important facilities." CBM is not removing infrastructure risk but shifts the risk within the Navy's bases and sites portfolio "to less important assets, short of failure" (CNIC, undated a). The CBM approach has a Navy watertight integrity theme, by focusing on building Enclosures first, then building Systems.

The CBM matrix is used to help develop requirements; see Figure 4.4 for an example of notional requirement amounts. Individual buildings are represented vertically and along the matrix rows based on facility importance as measured by the MDI score. MDI scores are grouped as follows: Critical (85–100), Significant (70–84), Relevant (55–69), Moderate (40–54), and Low (1–39). The building or other facility components are represented by the matrix columns, based on how critical they are following the watertight integrity theme: Enclosures, Systems, and Finishes. Enclosure items, such as roofs, walls, and windows, are considered critical building elements while System elements, such as electrical, mechanical, water, firefighting, and safety, are considered essential building elements (see Figure 4.5). We should note that

Figure 4.4
The Condition Based Maintenance Matrix with Notional Requirement Amounts for Buildings

Total Building Requirement	Critical		Essential				Low		
	Roofing	Walls, Windows, and Doors	Electrical	HVAC	Plumbing	Fire Protection	Interior Walls, Stairs, and Doors	Interior Finishes	Total
Critical	$129	$290	$ 451	$ 338	$139	$ 82	$108	$ 328	$1,866
Significant	$128	$239	$ 408	$ 341	$150	$102	$144	$ 323	$1,836
Relevant	$ 99	$191	$ 322	$ 280	$129	$ 64	$107	$ 262	$1,454
Moderate	$ 67	$108	$ 159	$ 129	$ 63	$ 32	$ 48	$ 134	$ 741
Low	$ 50	$105	$ 115	$ 89	$ 34	$ 13	$ 28	$ 99	$ 531
Total	$473	$934	$1,455	$1,177	$515	$293	$434	$1,147	$6,428

SOURCE: CNIC, undated a.

Figure 4.5
Diagram of Navy Installation Typical Building Components: Enclosures, Systems, and Finishes

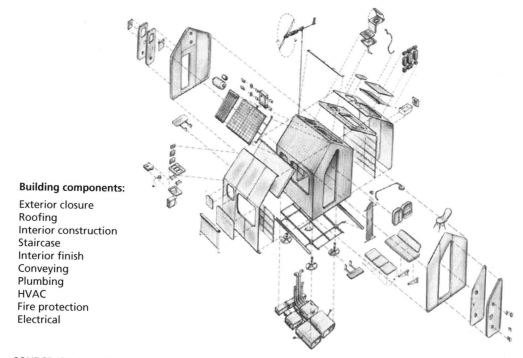

Building components:

Exterior closure
Roofing
Interior construction
Staircase
Interior finish
Conveying
Plumbing
HVAC
Fire protection
Electrical

SOURCE: CNIC, undated a.

a couple of people with Navy experience whom we interviewed suggested that the building Enclosure items should not be considered critical. They argued that personnel and facilities can tolerate leaks in windows and roofs, while an operational electrical system would be a higher priority as regards repairs.

These different component conditions are then applied to produce requirements in the CBM matrix. Requirements are generated based on the Condition Index of the components within the corresponding buildings. Requirements of the most critical buildings and components would be at the upper left of the matrix because they generate a higher Condition Index (85). The least critical buildings and components would be at the lower right, since they do not generate a requirement until the Condition Index drops to 50. This approach is applied across the matrix to identify requirements earlier for the critical items (CNIC, undated a).

The MDI is an important part of the CBM matrix and process. According to CNIC Instruction 11100.1A,

> The MDI is an operational risk metric describing the relative importance of shore facilities in terms of their mission criticality. MDI evaluates the installation's ability to support the Warfare Enterprise's mission should the infrastructure be damaged or destroyed. Inputs from operations personnel and tenant subject matter experts on the MDI process is required to best capture the operational mission impacts of facility degradation or outage. MDI is reported on a scale of 1 to 100 with 100 representing highest mission importance. (CNIC, 2018)

Figure 4.6 shows how buildings that contain functional activities that are most important for the Navy mission (such as communication centers, ship repair operations, and ordnance

Figure 4.6
The Navy Mission Dependency Index—Representative Facilities and Scores

Facility Criticality (MDI)	Buildings	Structures
Critical (85–100)	Communication center, air traffic control operations, major command admin, ship repair, BEQs (at training installation), and ordnance operations	Piers, wharves, primary runways, and major artery roads
Significant (70–84)	Ordnance storage, installation security, laboratory, CDC, BEQs, operations administration	Some wharves, secondary runways, taxiways, aprons
Relevant (55–69)	Academic instruction, some ordnance storage, warehousing	Taxiways, aprons, roads
Moderate (40–54)	MWR facilities, Navy Exchange, youth center, general administration, some ordnance storage	Some airfield pavement, small craft pier
Low (1–39)	MWR, general warehousing	Sidewalks, parking lots

SOURCE: CNIC, undated a.
NOTES: BEQs = Bachelor Enlisted Quarters; CDC = Child Development Center; MWR = Morale, Welfare and Recreation.

operations), are considered critical and have a higher MDI rating. Similarly, structures that are most important for the Navy mission (such as piers, wharves, and primary runways) are also considered critical, so they have higher MDI ratings. In contrast, facilities containing functional activities and structures that support functions that are considered not as significant to the Navy's mission receive lower MDI ratings.

The Navy targeted facilities investment strategy also states that SRM projects should be implemented when need has been determined by evidence from at least one of the following processes: "a) reliability analysis (e.g., preventive maintenance feedback), b) specialized inspections, or c) assessments (e.g., Infrastructure Condition Assessment Program)." Evidence of the need is supposed to be established before planned maintenance and repair projects are started. Installation "maintenance action plans and long-range maintenance plans will be developed and executed with this 'evidence-of-need,' prioritized approach" (Deputy Chief of Naval Operations for Fleet Readiness and Logistics, 2017).

The Navy's facility SRM requirements are supposed to be identified and budgeted with consideration for the facility condition with an emphasis on supporting "shore infrastructure needs directly affecting Navy Missions." Beginning in FY 2018, the Navy SRM program was resourced to prioritize the following requirements (in priority order):

1. Address life, health, and safety critical requirements
2. Conduct maintenance dredging where it directly supports fleet operations
3. Conduct breakdown maintenance where needed to support the continuation of operations
4. Conduct specialized inspections for critical infrastructure (e.g., bridges, dams, airfields, piers)
5. Conduct preventive maintenance for the purpose of maintaining equipment and facilities in a satisfactory operating condition
6. Address requirements in the Targeted Investment Focus Area (Deputy Chief of Naval Operations for Fleet Readiness and Logistics, 2017).

The Navy has a semiannual reporting system for its risk-based facilities investment strategy. Installations provide to the Navy Regions midyear information that is provided as regional reports by April 30. Then Naval Facilities Engineering Command provides all Budget Submitting Offices semiannual execution reports for validation before they are submitted to the CNIC. These midyear reports provide targeted investment plans and execution percentages (by dollar amount) for the first half of the current fiscal year by each Navy Region. These reports also include remedy plans for any Navy Region executing less than 75 percent in the targeted investment focus area. Such reports and their remedy plans help the Navy to adjust planned maintenance and repair investments part way through the year and makes sure that the funds are being spent appropriately on the targeted areas. Additionally, these reports provide targeted investment plan and execution data for other Budget Submitting Offices. Similarly, the Navy requires end of fiscal year reports that provide targeted investment plan and execution percentages (by dollar amount) by each Navy Region for the just completed fiscal year and the planned targeted investment percentages (by dollar amount) scheduled for the upcoming fiscal year by each Navy Region. Such reporting also provides targeted investment plan and execution data for other Budget Submitting Offices (Deputy Chief of Naval Operations for Fleet Readiness and Logistics, 2017).

Navy Uses of Software Tools to Help with Facility Sustainment

The Navy has been using Maximo and BUILDER to help with facility management and sustainment decisionmaking. Maximo is a commercial off-the-shelf facility management software system that is intended by the Navy to manage assets or equipment, not whole buildings.

Navy installations use Maximo to track daily facility sustainment work orders, including emergency repairs, routine service requests (such as light bulb replacements), and preventive maintenance. Installation PW staff do zone inspections on facilities using outstanding work request history for the facilities from Maximo. Navy personnel can also easily use Maximo to pull all the repair projects within the last year or more for any given installation facility. Navy installation PW staff also use the history of a building's maintenance projects from Maximo to show the CNIC the justification for upgrade or replacement funding.

CBM data has been captured in Maximo since FY 2017. In fact, for the CBM process, data input and management is in Maximo. However, this process is not "automated." It requires data entry and information management by Facilities Management Division personnel within each Public Works Department. There are three main steps for the CBM reporting process: (1) attaching the projects to the fiscal year Maintenance Execution Plan (one-year maintenance project plan); (2) relating the BUILDER generated requirements to the project; and (3) updating the project status in Maximo (CNIC, 2017).

The Navy started implementing BUILDER at its installations ten years ago, and all installations are using it. The Navy has the longest history with using BUILDER, but not every building at every installation has BUILDER data yet. The Navy uses BUILDER to help with preventive maintenance; it is used as a predictive tool to look ahead multiple years at potential facility repair needs. Navy installations use BUILDER to help predict and plan for repair investment funding out to five years to help with the 75 percent target levels and to develop special contract needs.

Installation PW personnel balance the different needs to create the facility sustainment project list. For instance, they balance emergency project needs with the commanders' requests and preventive maintenance needs. Preventive maintenance is identified using BUILDER to predict facility replacement needs. For example, installation personnel might run BUILDER to identify the most run-down buildings or that five buildings need roofs replaced during the next two years. For the latter need they may decide to do one larger roof replacement contract and achieve some economy of scale savings by repairing all five of the roofs together in that one contract.

Most Navy installations use a Work Induction Board to evaluate projects. Navy personnel put in for funding during the next fiscal year or other out-year plans. The bigger project jobs that require contractor help are tracked in the E-project database, such as roof or HVAC replacement.

U.S. Marine Corps Installation Facility Sustainment Practices

The Marine Corps manages 24 installations that are divided into three regions. Personnel at Marine Corps Installation Command told us that about 55 percent of the funding recommended by the FSM is delegated to individual installations. Funding for projects costing more than $300,000 is managed centrally, but the Marine Corps is planning to delegate more of the funding to the regions because of the administrative burdens of collecting information and deciding which projects to fund. Management personnel said that they were familiar with the Navy's CBM program, but they preferred to allow installations to determine which projects were the most critical to fund.

The Marine Corps funds a contractor team to perform BUILDER condition assessments across installations so that the data are consistent. They inspect about one-third of all facilities each year, except for facilities with special requirements that are inspected more frequently, such as bridges, dams, and airfields. The Marine Corps has reduced installation-level staffs that used to enter and analyze data, so they may not be getting as much value from systems like Maximo and BUILDER as they could. They are also not able to make as much use of equipment sensor data as the private sector does due to cybersecurity concerns.

The U.S. Marine Corps Forces Reserve

The U.S. Marine Corps Forces Reserve (MARFORRES) hired a contractor to perform facility condition assessments to input into BUILDER in 2013. In addition to facility condition assessments, the assessment teams concurrently performed space utilization studies, real property installed equipment inventories, and real property inventories. By performing all four assessments at once, MARFORRES saved time and money because of overlapping data requirements, such as equipment manufacturer, age, and capacity and area square footages. The assessment teams entered raw field data into BUILDER's remote entry database software either in real time, using computer tablets, or at the end of the day, based on an assessor's paper documentation. The building systems were rated using BUILDER's color condition rating system of green (good), amber (fair), and red (poor). When the teams encountered components that were not easily inspected or accessible, they rated the components using the program's age-based rating system, which extrapolates the condition of a component based solely on the type and age. Each site assessment took one to four days to complete, including quality assurance (Maguire and Hurd, 2018).

The contractor also held BUILDER training classes at each location to familiarize MARFORRES personnel with its terminology and processes and to demonstrate how field data was captured and entered into the database. MARFORRES plans to use BUILDER to create better forecasts of facility SRM costs and to transition from reactionary maintenance to a more proactive approach. It should also provide a more factual basis to justify SRM funding based on both mission criticality and economic efficiency. However, MARFORRES facility managers will need to learn to work directly with BUILDER and continuously update condition ratings as maintenance work is performed.

Air Force Installation Facility Sustainment Practices

Like the Army, Marine Corps, and Navy, the Air Force has also had challenges in being able to invest enough in facility sustainment.

Within the Air Force, all SRM funding goes to AFIMSC. AFIMSC retains about 50 percent of the funding, which is allocated to SRM projects using a centralized process managed by AFIMSC, and delegates the remainder of the funding to individual bases. The decentralized funding includes preventive maintenance and small repairs; it focuses on keeping the systems operating. The centralized funding is used to steer the overall portfolio and make strategic investment decisions.

A Centralized Process: The Comprehensive Asset Management Plan

The Air Force's centralized process uses the Air Force Comprehensive Asset Management Plan (AFCAMP) model to help develop a four-year Integrated Priority List (IPL) of projects based on the risk to mission and airmen across all bases.[3] Then the Air Force creates the Combined Tasking Order to prioritize larger SRM projects Air Force–wide.[4] The Air Force has been doing a risk-based management process for the centralized program for the last five years, and AFIMSC personnel reported that it has improved their ability to defend their budgets with senior leadership.

The centralized program used to do the "worst first" mission critical facilities. It incentivized installations to let facilities degrade to improve the score. Now the Air Force tries to tackle problems earlier, before they become more expensive to fix. It compared the "worst first" with what BUILDER recommended, and this showed that lower-priority facilities were going to fail over the next ten years, followed by maintenance shops, and so on. The Air Force built an Installation Health Assessment and showed how it changed with better planning of what to fix first. AFIMSC could provide the Air Force leadership with different scenarios of what would happen based on the funding provided. Using the Installation Health Assessment, AFIMSC showed that it did not need a huge amount of money to improve asset quality, but it needed to stop taking money out of SRM to fund other things. It could stop the growth of the sustainment backlog, reduce it, and eliminate it over 12 to 15 years.

The Air Force uses thresholds for its centralized funding process. R&M projects over $1 million or sustainment projects over $2 million are funded centrally. To obtain this funding, installations need to provide a validation worksheet with an analysis of alternatives and go through an asset management process to show that the project is needed. This involves more analysis and documentation than for decentralized projects. AFIMSC realized that when the threshold was too low, installations had to provide too much documentation for small projects. As a result, the Air Force made some exceptions to the requirements for some specialized projects that were not being funded locally, including projects with high savings to investment ratios, projects with matching funds, troop training projects, and so on. It provides some centralized funding for such projects. Some energy resiliency projects also fall into this category.

The Air Force Comprehensive Asset Management Plan Model

The AFCAMP model provides a simplified standardized risk assessment. It defines risk as the probability that something will fail multiplied by the consequence if it does fail. Specifically, Risk = POF × COF, where POF is the probability of failure and COF is the consequence of failure. The POF is an engineering assessment with values ranging from 1 to 100, using data

---

3   The Air Force's IPL used to be three years; it is four years for FY 2019, and will be five years for FY 2020.

4   The Combined Tasking Order is the execution year of the AFCAMP (which is the Air Force IPL). Execution year equals the Combined Tasking Order. IPL equals AFCAMP, which is the execution year plus three in FY 2019 and will be execution year plus four starting in FY 2020.

from SMSs and other sources (see Figure 4.7).[5] There are four sources for the POF: the Facilities Condition Index, Natural Infrastructure Index, the Pavement Condition Index, and the Utilities Condition Index. The Facilities Condition Index comes from BUILDER, and the Pavement Condition Index from PAVER. The Utilities Condition Index is not SMS based, but rather comes from the remaining service life based on the documented performance of breaks and outages. Natural infrastructure, such as stormwater management, is also included in this process and is based on the *Environmental Quality Programming Guide* (Air Force Civil Engineer Center [AFCEC], 2017).

COF is a mission impact assessment with values ranging from 1 to 100, and is calculated for both the built and natural infrastructure. For built infrastructure, the COF = MDI + Major Command (MAJCOM) mission impact. The MDI is 60 percent of the 100 points. Currently the Air Force assigns MDI based on the Category Code (CatCode) of the asset. However, it

Figure 4.7
The Air Force Comprehensive Asset Management Plan Model

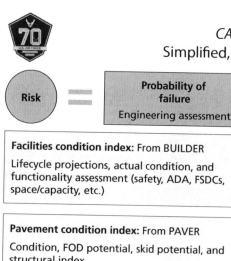

SOURCE: AFCEC, 2017.
NOTES: CAMP = (Air Force) Comprehensive Asset Management Plan; EQ = environmental quality; FOD = Foreign Object Debris; FSDCs = Fire Safety Deficiency Codes; PRV = plant replacement value.

---

[5] In 2018, for the FY 2019 AFCAMP, the Air Force launched a lowest-life-cycle model through which it moved away from the "worst first" approach because this allowed it to get after more requirements and thereby stretch its investment dollars further. As part of this process the Air Force made the adjustment to the maximum points on the POF side of the model; instead of having maximum points below 60, maximum points are now between 75 and 85.

found that buildings are not always being used for what they are coded for, and there are other problems with using the CatCode to determine the MDI, such as buildings with multiple uses. The Air Force is working on developing a tactical MDI that is similar to what the Navy uses so that it more accurately reflects the commander's mission priorities. The MAJCOM-defined mission impact accounts for exceptional requirements and issues that are not captured in the MDI, and it is 40 percent of the 100 points.

The Natural Infrastructure COF also comes from the *Environmental Quality Programming Guide*. It accounts for mission impact and risk related to public health and/or the environment and also includes stakeholders' concerns.

In the AFCAMP process, the Air Force gives special consideration to projects that are good investments (with a high savings-to-investment ratio).

The Integrated Priority List of Projects

Until 2019, the Air Force developed a three-year IPL—a single list of priorities for all projects across three fiscal years and all bases (see Figure 4.8). In 2019 the planning period was increased to four years, and it will be extended to five years in 2020. Projects are ranked based on the risk to mission and airmen across all bases. This process allows for a true multiyear IPL and improves the identification of candidate projects for design and execution in future years. It allows Air Force managers to give a "vector check" and validate the priorities year-round. The Installation Governance Structure approves the installation IPL. The installation IPLs are used to create the Combined Tasking Order to prioritize larger SRM projects Air Force–wide.

Figure 4.8
An Example of the Air Force Integrated Priority List as of 2017

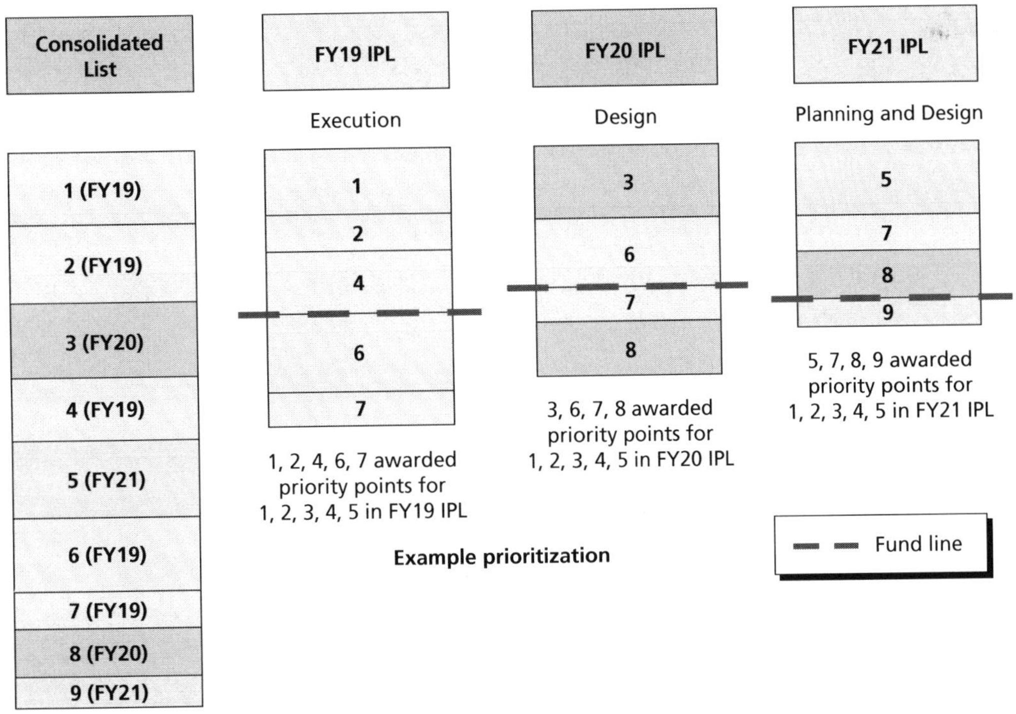

SOURCE: AFCEC, 2017.

The Decentralized Process Is Based on Installation Execution Plans

The decentralized part of the SRM budget goes to the bases, and each base develops an Execution Plan (for more information, see Horn, 2018). This plan is a comptroller-owned product covering all installation and mission support functions. It is a tool to predict, capture and validate requirements; integrate requirements and funding across the enterprise; and prioritize allocation of funding. However, it does not dictate how every dollar is spent and can be easily modified after approval. This Execution Plan includes all facility operations funds, including fire department operations. It also includes all in-house and base maintenance contracts, utilities and utility privatization costs, and the "big 3" (refuse removal, custodial operations, and grounds maintenance). Facility Operations does not include civilian salaries, it covers only equipment, utilities, and some other bills. The "big 3" and utility privatization are considered "must pay" bills. The majority of maintenance contracts and assessments and inspections are included in this decentralized program. For instance, maintenance contracts include those for elevators, cranes and hoists, boilers, chillers, overhead/hangar doors, hoods/ducts, fire suppression and alarms, and painting.

AFIMSC builds the first 80 percent of the Execution Plan for each base using SMS data from the bases, such as condition assessments from BUILDER and PAVER. Then bases add to and update their individual Execution Plans. This process is new in the past two years, because commands were merged. Installations used to run their own Execution Plans, which went up through the MAJCOMs; they were not standardized across installations, and each functional community worked through the MAJCOMs. Now the Air Force has centralized the installation management portion. It includes facility maintenance, work order supplies, equipment, small projects, and base operating support.

For the first time in 2018, AFIMSC created plans for each installation. It centralized the funding and the data management so that it can look across all the installations. AFIMSC wanted to establish some factors to distribute funding based on need and risk, and in 2018 it developed the plans based on data collected from the installations.[6] Ultimately, the Air Force wants to get to a risk-based model for decentralized funds, as well as centralized funds. According to AFIMSC, in summer 2018 the Air Force was about at the 80 percent solution. AFIMSC asks the installations to look at the plans and adjust them based on their local knowledge.

The Visible Asset Sustainment Tool

Every Air Force installation develops a sustainment plan for every real property asset over time, and they all use the Visible Asset Sustainment Tool (VAST) to develop the base plan. The plan is in an access database with detailed data for each asset. VAST data are developed with AFCEC and base inputs. First, VAST is prepopulated by AFCEC with unconstrained BUILDER data and shows the next seven years of requirements for each asset. Then each base fills in a three-year plan for each asset. VAST is used to help develop the base Execution Plan and also supplements data in that plan. VAST outputs dozens of useful reports for operations managers at the bases. For example, VAST produces reports to look across assets to see which supplies are needed and to see that in two years Building X will need $500,000 worth of repairs.

---

[6]   For FY 2019, AFIMSC is also leveraging BUILDER percent complete as a factor for funds distribution. The more the BUILDER data are complete, the more the BUILDER variable will contribute to funds distribution.

The Air Force Category Management Program

The Air Force is also implementing a category management (CM) program to improve its acquisition processes related to installation facility sustainment. CM is defined as

> [a] structured approach to create common categories of products and services that enables the Federal Government to eliminate redundancies, increase efficiency and effectiveness, and boost (customer) satisfaction with the products and services we deliver. (AFIMSC, undated, p. 6)

CM is a commercial best practice of strategic sourcing and supply chain management that has been used by companies such as Kroger, UPS, and Walmart to help reduce costs and improve effectiveness. The Air Force plans to apply it to installation facility sustainment such as roofing replacement and repair and elevator maintenance. For example, the Air Force issued a five-year, service-wide, indefinite-delivery, indefinite-quantity contract for roofing replacement and repair that resulted in savings and efficiencies of $12.07 million (27 percent) during the first one and a half years of implementation (AFIMSC, undated, p. 21).

Prior to introducing the CM approach for elevator maintenance, there was variation in pricing for maintenance and repair throughout the Air Force. There was no written guidance on maintenance standards, and as a result, the Air Force was paying for work that was above industry standards. The implementation of CM improved elevator maintenance practices by providing clear guidance and adopting a standardized Performance Work Statement based on a "full maintenance" standardized level of service that is aligned with industry standards (AFIMSC, undated, p. 6).

Army Reserve Component Facility Sustainment Practices

In this section we review some recent documents describing facility sustainment practices in the ARNG and USAR.

Army National Guard

In 2010 the Senate Armed Services Committee directed the ARNG to develop a nationwide capital investment strategy as part of Congressional Directive 111-201 (ARNG, 2014). As part of this effort, the ARNG created an Operational Readiness Index to establish a consistent methodology to develop all states' modernization plans and combine them into a national investment strategy. The Operational Readiness Index has two parts:

- The Stewardship Index combines traditional facility ratings based on the ISR FCI (Q ratings), the Space Utilization Index (C ratings), and functional capability ratings (F ratings).
- The MDI reflects the state's perspective regarding the "interruptability" and "relocatability" of the functions at each Readiness Center. The MDI represents the risk component of the facility to the ARNG mission and scores group facilities into three categories: mission critical, mission dependent, and mission support.[7]

---

7 Mission critical facilities (28 percent of nationwide ARNG facilities) are considered extremely difficult to replicate or relocate, such as Joint Forces Headquarters, brigade headquarters, or locations with unique unit requirements, such as aviation components; mission dependent facilities (36 percent) provide a variety of functional roles, may store significant quantities of equipment, and would be challenging to relocate; mission support facilities (36 percent) are commonly single-unit locations, or located away from target population centers. ARNG, 2014, pp. 42–43.

Based on these criteria, the ARNG developed a modernization plan that included retaining and improving 1,030 Readiness Center locations, consolidating 650 Readiness Center locations, and divesting 600 Readiness Center locations. It also developed an asset management modeling tool that incorporated physical degradation of facilities over time based on SRM funding levels, and a prioritization strategy for MILCON projects to show the effects of different SRM and MILCON funding levels over a 15-year time horizon in terms of the portfolio average Operational Readiness Index, facility condition ratings, and the Space Utilization Index. The effects of four projected funding scenarios are shown in Figure 4.9.[8]

Although ARNG SRM and MILCON funding appear to have increased since low points in FY 2015, it is not clear that the ARNG's Readiness Center Transformation Master Plan has

Figure 4.9
Relationship Between Funding Levels and the Operational Readiness Index

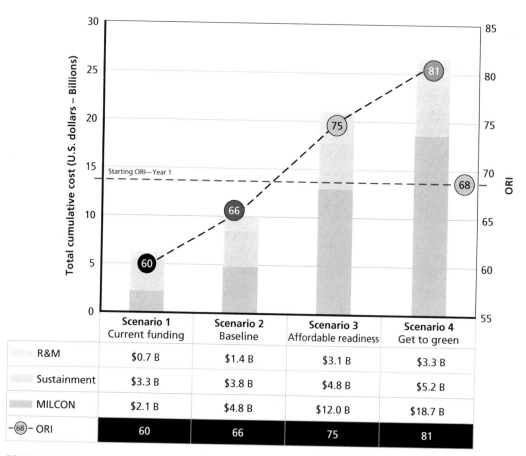

	Scenario 1 Current funding	Scenario 2 Baseline	Scenario 3 Affordable readiness	Scenario 4 Get to green
R&M	$0.7 B	$1.4 B	$3.1 B	$3.3 B
Sustainment	$3.3 B	$3.8 B	$4.8 B	$5.2 B
MILCON	$2.1 B	$4.8 B	$12.0 B	$18.7 B
ORI	60	66	75	81

SOURCE: ARNG, 2014, p. 71.
NOTE: ORI = Operational Readiness Index.

---

[8]   Sustainment funding is set at 65 percent of the FSM requirement in Scenario 1, 75 percent in Scenario 2, and 90 percent in Scenarios 3 and 4. Scenario 3 implements 53 percent of MILCON projects in the modernization plan, and Scenario 4 implements 100 percent.

resulted in significantly higher funding, since the budgets for the Army and the other services showed similar patterns.

U.S. Army Reserve

Thompson, Sorenson, and Buckrop (2018) discuss the process used by the USAR 88th Regional Support Command to conduct facility condition assessments for input into BUILDER across a 19-state region stretching from Ohio to Oregon and Washington. A joint venture among three firms conducted the assessments. The team first conducted pilot site surveys to visually inspect assets and standardize the data collection process. It placed bar code labels on each piece of equipment to facilitate future tracking. Each asset was rated according to the flowchart shown in Figure 4.10.

Thompson, Sorenson, and Buckrop's assessment of BUILDER is that it is a good tool for forecasting future workload, but it has only a limited ability to extract, display, and analyze data. It could also be improved by archiving historical data on facility conditions and repairs. In addition, BUILDER requires human intervention to validate data and ensure that it is updated after repairs are conducted.

Figure 4.10
The Standardized Rating Process Used by Contractors for the 88th Regional Support Command

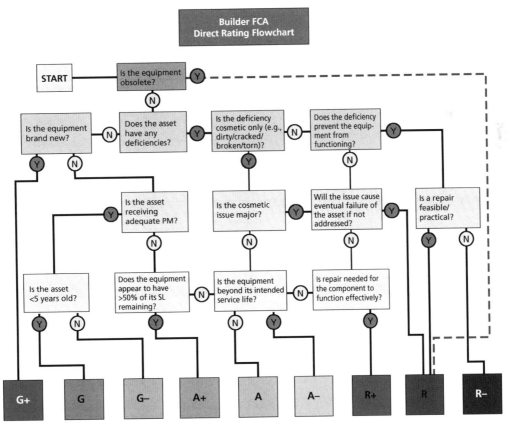

SOURCE: Thompson, Sorenson, and Buckrop, 2018.
NOTE: FCA = Facility Condition Assessment; PM = preventive maintenance; SL = service life.

The Proposed Army Mission Dependency Index

A study conducted by the U.S. Army Corps of Engineers' ERDC/CERL developed a methodology to create an MDI for Army facilities and tested the methodology at White Sands Missile Range with the help of Navy personnel who had been using the MDI approach. The study defines the MDI as follows:

> The MDI is an indicator of mission-related importance of installation building, facility and infrastructure elements to be used for the purpose of providing more effective local prioritization of facilities for sustainment, restoration, and modernization (SRM) actions. (Grussing et al., 2010, p. ii)

The MDI was originally developed by the Coast Guard and the Navy, and has also been implemented by the Air Force and the National Aeronautics and Space Administration.

The information needed to calculate the MDI is generated through interviews with operational commanders and facility managers. The first step in creating the MDI is to categorize the missions performed at the installation and link the specific buildings and other support structures to each mission. These include both tenant missions and functions provided by the installation, such as operating forces support, community support, and base support. For each facility, an interview process is used to determine the facility's "interruptability," which measures how long functions supported by the facility could be stopped without adverse impact on the mission, and its "relocatability," which measures whether the mission could be relocated to other fixed or temporary facilities. Table 4.3 summarizes the ratings that are used to categorize the interruptability and relocatability of a facility.

The mission dependency score for facilities directly related to the mission is calculated based on the interruptability and relocatability ratings, as shown in Figure 4.11.

After the facilities associated with each mission are evaluated, mission interdependencies, defined as the indirect effects of other facilities not directly related to the mission that provide

Table 4.3
Interruptability and Relocatability Ratings

Interruptability	Relocatability
I = Immediate (functions performed in the facility must be maintained continuously)	I = Impossible (an alternate location is not available)
U = Urgent (minutes, not to exceed 1 hour)	X = Extremely Difficult (alternate location exists with minimally acceptable capabilities, but would require significant resources or dislocation of another tenant)
B = Brief (hours, not to exceed 24 hours)	
S = Short (days, not to exceed 7 days)	V = Very Difficult (an alternate location with marginally acceptable capabilities, but would require significant resources or dislocation of another tenant
P = Prolonged (weeks, not to exceed 1 month)	
E = Extended (1–6 months, up to 1 week to make operational)	D = Difficult (an alternate location with acceptable capabilities but would require unbudgeted resources)
F = Future (6 months to 2 years, up to 1 month to make operational)	P = Possible (an alternate location is readily available with sufficient capabilities and capacity, and requires no additional resources)
M = Mothballed (2+ years, up to several months to make operational)	
D = Demolish	

SOURCE: Grussing et al., 2010.

Figure 4.11
The Mission Dependency Scoring Matrix

MDw		MISSION INTRA-DEPENDENCY SCORE										
		Q1: Interruptability										
		Immediate (24/7)	Urgent (min/hr)	Brief (hrs/day)	Short (days/week)	Prolonged (week/month)	Extended (1–6 months)	Future (6 mo–2 yrs)	Mothball (2+ years)	Historical	Abandoned	Turn-in demo'd
Q2: Relocatability	Impossible	80	78	74	68	60	50	40	30	1.5	1	0
	Extremely difficult	76	72	66	58	48	38	28	20	1.5	1	0
	Very difficult	70	64	56	46	36	26	18	12	1.5	1	0
	Difficult	62	54	44	34	24	16	10	6	1.5	1	0
	Possible	52	42	32	22	14	8	4	2	1.5	1	0

SOURCE: Grussing et al., 2010.
NOTE: MDw = Mission dependency within a functional element.

Figure 4.12
The Mission Interdependency Scoring Matrix

MISSION INTER-DEPENDENCY SCORE							
MDb		Q3: Interruptability					
		None (24/7)	Urgent (min/hr)	Brief (hrs/day)	Short (days/week)	Prolonged (week/month)	Extended (1–6 months)	Future (6 mo–2 yrs)
Q4: Relocatability	Impossible	20	18	16	14	12	10	8
	Extremely difficult	18	16	14	12	10	8	6
	Very difficult	16	14	12	10	8	6	4
	Difficult	14	12	10	8	6	4	2
	Possible	12	10	8	6	4	2	0

SOURCE: Grussing et al., 2010.
MDb = Mission dependency between functional elements.

essential operational support or services, must be assessed. The same set of interruptability and relocatability ratings are applied to the availability of the operational support services provided by other functional areas on the installation. The mission interdependency score is calculated as shown in Figure 4.12.

The overall MDI score is based on the sum of the mission dependency score (maximum value of 80) and the average of the mission interdependency scores for other missions or functional areas that depend on the same facilities (maximum value of 20). Thus, the result ranges between 0 and 100. An overall MDI score of 80–100 is considered critical, 60–79 is significant, 35–59 is relevant, 15–34 is moderate, and 0–14 is low. The MDI score can be used to prioritize SRM funding to mission critical facilities, or to identify low-scoring facilities for potential divestiture or demolition, particularly if the building is in poor condition. MDI scores can also be entered into BUILDER to be used in conjunction with the FCI to link the probability of infrastructure failure with the severity of the consequences of a failure.

ERDC/CERL estimated that it would cost $40,000 to $75,000 per Army installation to conduct MDI assessments, but these costs could be reduced by combining the collection of MDI interruptability and relocatability with the ISR-I inspection process. This approach would require some additional training of the assessors who conduct ISR-I inspections.

Conclusions

In recent years, the Army's funding of SRM as a percentage of the requirements estimated by the FSM has been comparable to that of the other services. However, Army MILCON funding to replenish facilities has fallen below that of the other services, and it has also been slower to implement BUILDER, which is required by DoD policy.

The Navy, Marine Corps, and Air Force follow different processes for allocating facility sustainment funding to installations. The Navy allocates almost all SRM funding to installations but sets centralized priorities. It uses a CBM model to direct 75 percent of planned SRM projects to Targeted Investment Focus Areas, including critical or significant facilities, based on an MDI and critical building elements, such as roofs, electrical and mechanical systems, and safety requirements. The Marine Corps delegates about 55 percent of the funding recommended by the FSM to installations. Funding for sustainment projects costing more than $300,000 is managed centrally, but the Marine Corps is considering delegating more of this funding to the regional level to reduce administrative burdens. Unlike in the Navy, Marine Corps managers preferred to allow installations to determine which projects were the most critical to fund.

The Air Force delegates about half of SRM funding to installations for preventive maintenance and minor repairs, and the remainder is allocated to projects using a centralized process. The Air Force uses the AFCAMP model to develop a four-year IPL of projects across installations. AFIMSC is also developing a more centralized process to develop installation sustainment plans using condition assessments from BUILDER and PAVER. In addition, it is using CM to standardize service contracts, such as those for roofing replacement and repair and elevator maintenance, and to obtain economies of scale cost savings.

CHAPTER FIVE

Insights from Facility Management Trends, Practices, and Research

In this chapter we discuss our findings from a review of some relevant facilities management literature that is aimed primarily at non-DoD public- and private-sector organizations. We focused on sources that discussed how to improve facility sustainment practices and measure performance.

The Facility Management Framework

All organizations that maintain physical facilities, regardless of the organizational goals, have the same general concerns when managing a facility. Depending on the organization's priorities, facility management can seek to prioritize cost (including avoiding penalty costs associated with equipment breakdowns), reliability and ability to meet mission needs, safety, environmental concerns, or other mandates (National Research Council, 1996). There are trade-offs among these factors; for example, a facility can have high functional reliability with rapid facilities management response time, but maintaining a facility at that level may be expensive. A less costly management system may be less reliable or have a slower response time. Deciding between these trade-offs is the responsibility of facilities managers developing management plans.

One example of such a trade-off is the choice to defer maintenance in favor of cost savings in the present. While this approach may be financially appealing in the short term, deferring maintenance can increase costs over time and reduce the reliability and performance of a system below acceptable standards. The impacts of deferred maintenance are illustrated in Figure 5.1.

Therefore, sources such as Lewis and Payant (2007) recommend that facility sustainment should be integrated with other facility management functions, including facility planning; engineering and design of new facilities, modifications to facilities, and repair projects; construction of facilities and installation of equipment, including the selection of HVAC systems; and evaluation of facility or equipment replacement projects that are intended to save maintenance or utility costs. The overall goal should be to minimize the life-cycle costs of construction, operations and maintenance, and eventual disposal or replacement of facilities. While Army installation DPWs control some of these functions, funding tends to be stovepiped or constrained, so that it may be difficult to consider trade-offs between costs at different phases of the facility life cycle. In particular, construction design and funding are separated from other aspects of facility management. In addition, constraints on facility SRM funding may lead to deferred maintenance or repair that increases the risk and costs of equipment breakdowns.

Figure 5.1
Deferred Facility Maintenance May Cause Lost Service Utility of Equipment

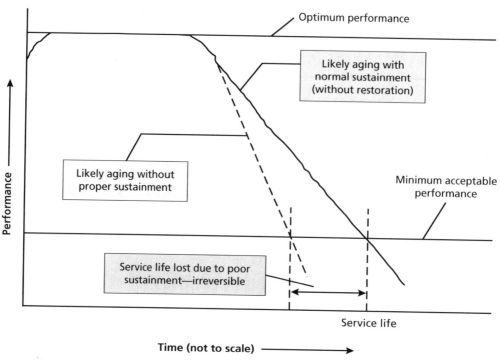

SOURCE: Deputy Under Secretary of Defense (Installations), 2001.

Facility Management Strategies

Many public-sector organizations find it difficult to implement a facility management strategy that minimizes life-cycle costs, because the annual budgeting process may not consider the long-term costs of deferring maintenance. For example, the National Research Council (1996) describes four levels of facility management strategies, which are summarized in Table 5.1. We discuss each level in more detail in the following paragraphs.

Basic strategies: Basic strategies include a combination of run-to-failure or breakdown maintenance and preventive maintenance (National Research Council, 1996). Run-to-failure or breakdown maintenance means that facilities or equipment are only repaired when a problem is reported. Run-to-failure maintenance ensures that equipment or components are not replaced until they wear out or fail, but it can also create inefficiencies for the facility or system if a broken component cannot be replaced quickly. Additionally, budgeting for labor and costs is difficult, as run-to-failure maintenance is highly unpredictable.

Basic preventive maintenance involves regularly scheduled replacement of components with known life spans, such as replacing HVAC filters once a month. The benefits of basic preventive maintenance include a clear and predictable timeline for labor and parts requirements; fewer equipment failures; and the ability to plan for downtime that would affect the facility's tenants and their productivity (Lewis and Payant, 2007, Chapter 5). SchoolDude, a provider of operations and maintenance and energy management software for schools and universities, found that customer organizations that completed more than 90 percent of preventive

Table 5.1
Categories of Facility Management Strategies

Level	Description of Strategy
Basic	Combination of • Run-to-failure/breakdown maintenance • Preventive maintenance
Intermediate	• Predictive testing and inspection: monitor operating parameters to detect excessive wear or impending failure • Condition survey inspections and condition assessments (for long-range planning)
More advanced	• Programmed maintenance/reliability-centered maintenance: optimize periodic maintenance to improve reliability and reduce life-cycle costs
Most advanced	• Predictive modeling: identify future maintenance requirements by facility, system, or component

SOURCE: National Research Council, 1996.

maintenance tasks had 28 to 39 percent lower average costs per work order and reduced the number of emergency repairs by more than half. In addition, it found that every $1 in deferred maintenance on roofs and HVAC systems resulted in $3 to $4 higher maintenance costs in the future. Proper preventive maintenance extended the lives of these major building components by 30 percent.[1]

Koo (2002) and Koo and Van Hoy (undated) estimated the net present value and ROI of preventive maintenance based on cost data for a telecommunications firm. The data were collected through a survey of 12 percent of the company's real estate portfolio of 119 million sq ft, including the type and age of equipment and annual preventive maintenance expenditures on each type of equipment. At the portfolio level, the analysis indicated that a preventive maintenance program costing $39 million per year had a net present value of $2 billion over a 25-year period and a ROI of 545 percent. Most of the savings came from extending the useful life of equipment, with energy savings accounting for about 7 percent of the benefits.

However, a potential drawback to replacing components on a fixed schedule is that some parts are replaced before they have reached the end of their useful lives. Thus, higher-level strategies combine regularly scheduled preventive maintenance with predictive testing, inspections, and modeling. Based on survey data collected in a manufacturing setting, Swanson (2001) found that a combination of preventive and predictive maintenance was associated with higher product quality, better equipment availability, and lower production costs relative to reactive maintenance.

Intermediate strategies: Intermediate strategies include condition surveys and assessments and predictive testing and inspection (National Research Council, 1996). Condition surveys are conducted by trained professionals who assess the condition of a facility or component based on a rating scale that is objective, repeatable, and sensitive enough to measure deterioration rates. The frequency of inspection depends on the facility type and use; the system, component, or material type; the current condition; and the rate of deterioration. Based on these factors, reinspection should occur every one to five years. Condition surveys are used to inform managers of system conditions and develop mid- to long-range plans based on reasonable predictions on which parts will need replacement and on what timeline.

---

[1] SchoolDude, 2013. The same study found that an effective preventive maintenance program reduced energy costs and was associated with lower insurance claims.

Predictive testing and inspection monitors the condition and performance of facilities systems and equipment to detect trends or conditions that indicate excessive wear or impending failure. Techniques include vibration monitoring, measuring equipment temperature using infrared thermography, oil analysis to detect contaminants or wear particles, and ultrasound to detect high-frequency noise caused by leaks in pressurized systems (Lewis and Payant, 2007, Chapter 5). Predictive testing and inspection may involve embedded sensors, online systems, or portable systems for periodic readings, and this technology is often intended to be used with a CMMS system (National Research Council, 1996). This approach can allow for just-in-time repairs, which should decrease downtime associated with system failures. The sensors and software needed for predictive testing can require a significant up-front investment and may not be a viable option for industries in which cybersecurity is a concern.

More advanced strategies: More advanced facilities maintenance strategies include programmed maintenance and reliability-centered maintenance (National Research Council, 1996). Programmed maintenance can be used for facilities, systems, or components whose failure is less critical, such as pavement seal coats, roof drainage system cleaning, and painting, and when the proper frequency can be determined with a high degree of confidence. Programmed maintenance generally means that fewer replacements are scheduled than with basic preventive maintenance, but it requires highly accurate and detailed data inputs, which can be labor intensive to gather.

Reliability-centered maintenance combines the most cost-effective mix of breakdown maintenance, preventive maintenance, predictive testing and inspection, and proactive maintenance based on nondestructive and noninvasive testing to determine the need for maintenance or replacement of components (National Research Council, 1996). Proactive maintenance includes the use of total quality management techniques to identify the root causes of failures and take corrective actions to gain the full expected life of other similar components. A reliability-centered maintenance approach can be adjusted to prioritize cost savings, reliability, labor requirements or other variables, depending on the organizational priorities.

The most advanced strategy: The most advanced strategy is predictive modeling, which uses historic data to anticipate and schedule future maintenance requirements by facility, system, or component (National Research Council, 1996). Predictive modeling requires a significant amount of data input into the model, and the model itself can require sophisticated analysis. Predictive modeling can be exceptionally useful, however, for situations in which facilities maintenance budgets are prepared years in advance. A typical budget is created for future needs based on current conditions; predictive modeling allows for more accurate budget predictions within the anticipated timeline.

Additionally, as facilities degrade, the cost to restore them increases curvilinearly (National Research Council, 1996). This means that there is an optimal time to replace parts or perform maintenance; being able to predict this timeline and then following the schedule will result in lowest costs, highest reliability, and the best condition for the facility.

A second interpretation of different levels of facility maintenance strategies is given in Table 5.2, based on information from the National Center for Education Statistics (2006). This matrix is useful because it relates the maintenance strategy to the budget, the share of preventive versus corrective maintenance, reliability, customer service and satisfaction, and the FCI.

Organizations that are able to achieve higher-level facility management strategies typically have lower life-cycle costs, but implementation of these strategies requires accurate data and more complex plans and modeling. Most organizations use CMMSs to track mainte-

Table 5.2
Facilities Condition Levels of Maintenance

Level	1	2	3	4	5
Description	Showpiece Facility	Comprehensive Stewardship	Managed Care	Reactive Management	Crisis Response
Maintenance budget as % of PRV	>4.0	3.5–4.0	3.0–3.4	2.5–2.9	<2.5
Preventive vs. corrective maintenance	100%	75–99%	50–74%	25–49%	<25%
Maintenance mix	All recommended preventive maintenance is scheduled and performed on time. Reactive maintenance is minimized to the unavoidable or economical. Emergencies are very infrequent and handled efficiently.	A well-developed preventive maintenance program: most required preventive maintenance is done at a frequency slightly less than per defined schedule. Appreciable reactive maintenance required due to systems wearing out prematurely. Occasional emergencies caused by component failures.	Reactive maintenance predominates due to systems failing to perform. Effort to schedule preventive maintenance: as time and manpower permit. The high number of emergency repairs causes reports to upper administration.	Worn-out systems require manpower to be scheduled to react to systems that are performing poorly or not at all. Significant time spent procuring parts and services due to the high number of emergency situations. Preventive maintenance consists of simple tasks and is done inconsistently.	No preventive maintenance performed due to more pressing problems. Reactive maintenance is a necessity due to worn-out systems. Good emergency response because of skills gained in reacting to frequent system failures.
Building systems' reliability	Breakdown maintenance is rare and limited to vandalism and abuse repairs.	Breakdown maintenance is limited to system components short of mean time between failures.	Building and systems components periodically or often fail.	Many systems unreliable. Constant need for repair. Backlog of repair needs exceeds resources.	Many systems nonfunctional. Repair only instituted for life safety issues.
Customer service and response time	Able to respond to virtually any type of service; immediate response.	Response to most service needs is typically in a week or less.	Services available only by reducing maintenance, with response times of 1 month or less.	Services available only by reducing maintenance, with response times of 1 year or less.	Services not available unless directed from top administration; none provided except in emergencies.
Customer satisfaction	Proud of facilities, have a high level of trust for the facilities' organization.	Satisfied with facilities-related services, usually complimentary of facilities staff.	Accustomed to basic level of facilities care. Generally able to perform mission duties. Lack of pride in physical environment.	Generally critical of cost, responsiveness, and quality of facilities services.	Consistent customer ridicule, mistrust of facilities services.
Service efficiency	Maintenance activities appear highly organized and focused. Equipment and building components are fully functional and regularly upgraded, keeping them current with modern standards and usage.	Maintenance activities appear organized with direction. Equipment and building components are usually functional and regularly upgraded, keeping them current with modern standards and usage.	Maintenance activities appear to be somewhat organized but remain people dependent. Equipment and building components are mostly functional, and equipment is periodically upgraded to current standards and use.	Maintenance activities appear somewhat chaotic and are people dependent. Equipment and building components are frequently broken and inadequate to meet present use needs.	Maintenance activities appear chaotic and without direction. Equipment and building components are routinely broken and inadequate to meet present use needs.

Table 5.2—Continued

Level	1	2	3	4	5
Description	Showpiece Facility	Comprehensive Stewardship	Managed Care	Reactive Management	Crisis Response
Average FCI	<0.05	0.05–0.15	0.16–0.29	0.30–0.49	≥0.50

SOURCE: National Center for Education Statistics, 2006.

NOTES: FCI $= \frac{\text{Deferred Maintenance}}{\text{Current Replacement Value}}$. FCI is the inverse of the U.S. Army's Quality Score (QS). QS $= 1 - \frac{\text{Deferred Maintenance}}{\text{Current Replacement Value}}$. PRV = plant replacement value

nance requests, schedule preventive maintenance, prepare budget estimates, and project facilities maintenance requirements. Lewis and Payant (2007, Chapter 2) describe some of the key features of a good CMMS. The basic types of information required are

- facility information, where a facility is defined as a logical grouping of equipment, such as a building, plant, or other structure
- equipment information, including major components or subassemblies
- maintenance procedures, which describe what must be done to equipment at a given time, with a level of detail based on the needs of the organization and the skills of equipment maintenance personnel
- calendar information, including the frequency of maintenance procedures (daily, monthly, etc.) and a scheduling routine
- parts, supplies, and tools needed for each maintenance procedure.

To meet the needs of facility managers and maintenance personnel, CMMS software should be easy to use, logically formatted, and fast-operating. From a management perspective, it should be capable of sorting information in many different ways and generating routine management information (such as cost, workforce, and equipment performance data) as well as customer reports. Lewis and Payant also note, "There are a few general ledger programs which have a 'maintenance module.' However, such programs are generally written by programmers concerned with accounting who are not familiar with the practical aspects of performing maintenance" (2007, p. 2.10). They recommend that it is typically better to use a system that is specifically designed for facility maintenance and transfer the data that is needed by the accounting program.

Comparison with Army Policies Regarding Facilities Management Strategies

Based on IMCOM policy guidance on developing AWPs and our observations at the installations we visited, the Army's facility management strategy is mainly at a basic to intermediate level. Recommended allocations of facility SRM funding are shown in Table 5.3, which is comparable to the basic level of maintenance in Table 5.1 or reactive management in Table 5.2. However, the use of condition survey inspections and condition assessments, as in the ISR-I, is at the intermediate level in Table 5.1. Some installations are finding difficulties entering the required data into GFEBS to generate preventive maintenance work orders, which suggests that they are at the "crisis response" level in Table 5.2. The Army's implementation of BUILDER offers an opportunity to create the initial data needed to move toward a predictive modeling strategy, but a long-term approach is needed to update facility condition information over time and integrate it with the annual work planning process.

Table 5.3
Army Directorate of Public Works Annual Work Plan Funding Prioritization

Percentage of Funding	Allocation	Description
30	Preventive maintenance orders	• Supports high-performance-sustainable buildings • Reduces emergencies and corrective maintenance demands
50	Sustainment (demand maintenance orders)	• Priority 1: Emergency, life/health/safety • Priority 2: Urgent (could become emergency if uncorrected) • Priority 3: Routine
15	Sustainment projects	• Major component repairs and replacements
5	Garrison-level migration to R&M projects	• Restoration: repair and replacement work to restore facilities damaged by inadequate sustainment, excessive age, natural disaster, fire, accident, or other causes • Modernization: alteration of facilities to implement new or higher standards, to accommodate new functions

SOURCE: Kuhr and Carr, 2017.

Facilities Management Performance Metrics

An additional method to assess facilities management is the utilization of metrics, which help managers quantify and track changes in facilities condition over time. Performance measurement is the process of reviewing past and current functioning of a facility and comparing performance among facilities to provide direction for decisionmaking. Performance metrics can be used both to evaluate changes in an individual facility's status over time and to compare the status of similar buildings. They can also be used to understand the impacts of management decisionmaking on the success and failure of a portfolio of facilities and to suggest possible improvements.[2]

Lavy, Garcia, and Dixit (2010) surveyed the literature on facility performance indicators, including published books, articles in peer-reviewed journals and conference proceedings, and benchmarking surveys. They identified a total of 35 performance metrics and grouped them into four categories:

1. financial indicators, which track costs and expenditures associated with operation and maintenance, energy, building functions, and other factors
2. physical indicators, which assess the physical shape and condition of the facility or building and its systems and components
3. functional indicators, which describe how the facility or building functions and its appropriateness for the desired purpose, such as space adequacy, availability of parking, and effects on employee productivity and turnover, and long-term business or organizational goals
4. survey-based indicators, which are based on respondents' opinions and are primarily qualitative in nature.

---

[2] See Lavy and Dixit, 2017; Lavy, Garcia, and Dixit, 2010, 2014a, 2014b; and Lavy, Garcia, Scinto, and Dixit, 2014.

In later work, Lavy, Garcia, and Dixit (2014a; 2014b) sought to identify a concise list of four to six performance metrics that would provide a holistic assessment of facility performance, including both financial and nonfinancial aspects; that were quantifiable and measurable; and that were applicable to a wide range of facilities or projects. Based on interviews with industry representatives and criteria such as eliminating redundancy, availability of data, ease of data collection and interpretation, and factors that can be controlled by facility managers, they identified four key performance indicators:

- $\text{FCI} = 1 - \dfrac{\textit{Deferred Maintenance}}{\textit{Current Replacement Value}}$

- $\text{Maintenance Efficiency Indicator} = \dfrac{\textit{Actual Spending on Deferred Maintenance}}{\textit{Total Deferred Maintenance}} \div \textit{Condition Index}$

- $\text{Replacement Efficiency Indicator} = \dfrac{\textit{Actual Replacement Spending}}{\textit{Cost of Replacing Expired Systems}}$

- $\text{Functional Index} = \dfrac{\textit{Actual Area of Specific Space Type}}{\textit{Required Area of Specific Space Type}}.$

The FCI, which is defined based on the ratio of the costs of deferred maintenance to the current replacement value of the facility or system, is used by many organizations (including the Army) to assess facility condition and to aid in the capital planning process. It is sometimes defined as above, with 100 indicating the best condition, or simply as the ratio of deferred maintenance to replacement value, where values close to 0 indicate the best condition. The Maintenance Efficiency Indicator measures how much of the backlog of deferred maintenance is completed relative to the facility's condition index. For example, to maintain an FCI of 80 percent, the organization must complete 80 percent of required maintenance each year. In this case, the maintenance efficiency indicator equals 1. To improve the FCI, the maintenance efficiency indicator must be greater than 1, whereas if it falls below 1, the FCI will deteriorate.

The Replacement Efficiency Indicator focuses on the percentage of expired systems (such as roofs or HVAC systems that have reached the end of their economically useful lives) that are replaced each year. These expenditures are classified as capital renewal rather than system maintenance. A value of 1 indicates that all expired systems are replaced, whereas a value less than 1 indicates that the organization has not replaced all expired systems in the facility. Finally, the functional index measures the amount of different types of facility space available relative to requirements. It can be calculated at various levels, including specific types of space within a building or as a weighted average for a building or portfolio of facilities as a whole. The higher-level indexes can help identify deficiencies that can be addressed by reconfiguring existing space rather than constructing new space.

These equations and metrics are useful not only for facilities managers to track facilities conditions within their garrisons, but also for headquarters management to track facilities conditions among Army bases worldwide.

Facilities Maintenance Prioritization Tools

As discussed above, there are a number of tools available to allow facilities managers to assess and track the condition of their facilities. Grussing, Uzarski, and Marrano (2006) describe how these metrics can be combined with financial analysis and information on component deterioration trends to set repair priorities and reduce life-cycle ownership costs. For example, when the condition index for a system or component falls below a predetermined threshold, the ROI of various maintenance approaches can be compared. A ROI considers trade-offs between up-front repair or replacement costs and overall life-cycle costs of the system based on its effects on system performance and future repair and replacement costs. Depending on the type of system the following options can be compared:

- Run to failure: If no corrective action is taken, the component's performance will degrade to a point where it fails and must be replaced, resulting in future costs and possible disruption to mission.
- Stopgap repair: Measures can be taken to slow or halt degradation until a more permanent solution can be accomplished, thus deferring the cost of a major repair or replacement for a short period of time.
- Major corrective repair: Major repairs may not restore the component to like-new condition but could extend its service life and defer the capital cost of replacement.
- Replacement: The component's condition is restored to its maximum value and its service life is reset. Replacement may also involve some modernization, which could lead to lower maintenance or energy costs.

Across a portfolio of facilities, this approach can be used to prioritize repairs and replacements based on the expected ROI of each project. The organization can also consider the importance of the building or component based on a Component Importance Index that measures the impact of the repair on the risk of system failure or an MDI that measures the importance of the building with respect to the organization's mission. By assigning relative weights to these factors, a consistent and repeatable importance score can be calculated for each project and used to set priorities under a limited maintenance budget.

Willman (2019) also argues that demonstrating the net present value of repairs or replacement of critical equipment is important for justifying the facility sustainment budget to higher management. For example, the Office of Facility Management at the U.S. State Department, which is responsible for maintenance and repair budgets for overseas embassies, developed a spreadsheet template for future-year annual budget submissions to be used by the facility management staff at each embassy. The spreadsheet showed the impacts of planned projects on sustainment costs over a five-year time horizon and was rolled up in the CMMS at the headquarters of the Office of Facility Management to develop a proposed budget. This approach also allows comparisons between similar embassies in regions that have comparable climates and local resources. In addition, Willman recommends that facility sustainment costs should be reported to higher management at least twice a month to capture the costs of unexpected equipment breakdowns and emergencies.

At the more advanced level, predictive modeling can be used to show the effects of different funding levels on facility conditions over time. For example, ERDC/CERL has developed the IMPACT simulation model, which can be used in conjunction with BUILDER data, to show the effects of facilities maintenance budgets and prioritization strategies on facility condition and costs up to ten years into the future. The model inputs include the real property inventory, condition information and deterioration trends, current work projects, budget projections, and user-defined standards, policies, and prioritization strategies. The model then generates work requirements based on projected conditions, prioritizes work projects, assigns funding to the highest-priority projects within the projected budget, and predicts the future condition of the component inventory based on the work completed and deferred. The outputs of the model allow decisionmakers to see the effects of budgets and policies on the condition of facilities over time and make adjustments to improve performance and ROI (Grussing, Uzarski, and Marrano, 2006, pp. 5–6).

Facilities Management Research Trends

Brochner (2017) examined trends in facility management research based on eight review articles published between 2013 and 2017. One important trend in facilities management research is looking at the link between people, the jobs they do, and the space they work in. The International Standards Organization (ISO) standard 41011:2017 defines facility management as a function that "integrates *people, place and process* within the built environment with the purpose of improving the quality of life of people and the productivity of the core business." ISO's technical committee for facility management is also developing additional standards for development of a facility management strategy (ISO/AWI 41014) and influencing behaviors for improved facility outcomes and user experience (ISO/AWI 41015). Existing standards indicate that facility management activities should be aligned with the demand organization's mission and core business objectives and prioritized based on their contributions to those objectives, such as improving patient care in a hospital. In addition, facility managers should be able to demonstrate how sustainment activities support the parent organization's objectives (Martin and Deckert, 2019).

Other recent research is examining the link between facility condition, office design, and environmental conditions (such as thermostat setting) with absenteeism, employee satisfaction, and productivity. For example, De Been and Beijer (2014) and Van der Voordt (2004) examined the effects of office design (individual, shared, and flexible/combined office spaces) on employee satisfaction and productivity. Other innovations include the use of data on things such as room occupancy, movements of building occupants, and energy use to design workspaces, enhance services, and reduce costs.[3] Brown et al. (2014) used body sensors to track face-to-face interactions between individuals to measure the effects of an office redesign.

Lister (2019) points out that in most organizations, personnel costs are much higher than facility costs. Thus, designing and maintaining facilities that have positive effects on productivity, employee turnover, and absenteeism can have a much greater impact on the organization's success than can reducing facility sustainment costs. For example, the costs of employee turnover range from about 16 percent of salary for the lowest-paid workers to over 200 percent for the most highly paid and skilled workers. The Centers for Disease Control and Prevention and the General Services Administration have also developed standards and evidence-based

---

[3]   See Adama and Michell, 2017; Maglio and Lim, 2016; and Sailer, Pomeroy, and Haslem, 2015.

health metrics to measure how well facilities promote employee health and well-being and identify enhancements that would have the greatest impact on occupants. The Fitwell Certification System has a web portal that allows facility managers to assess which standards are currently being met and assign a numerical score to buildings that can be improved over time by implementing incremental changes (Agarwal and Karerat, 2019).

A GAO study on defense facility condition interviewed PW personnel and conducted focus groups at eight U.S. military installations, including two Army installations, Aberdeen Proving Ground, Maryland, and Fort Leavenworth, Kansas (GAO, 2016, pp. 3, 24–30). They found that the condition of facilities can have both positive and negative effects on quality of life. Personnel expressed satisfaction with facilities that were new or recently renovated, but they also reported problems with malfunctioning HVAC systems, leaking roofs and windows, and mold and mildew in installation facilities; these had negative effects on quality of life at military installations. In some cases these problems caused property damage or health effects or required personnel to be moved to other facilities.

The general trend in facilities management research is to recognize that the environment in which people perform their work has an impact on productivity, work quality, and quality of life. Thus, underfunding maintenance of Army facilities could be having negative effects on productivity and retention of both military and civilian personnel.

Conclusions

Private-sector organizations tend to focus on minimizing the life-cycle costs of facility ownership, including construction, operation and maintenance, and eventual disposal or replacement of facilities. Advanced facility management strategies include optimizing preventive maintenance to improve reliability and reduce life-cycle costs and use of predictive modeling to identify future maintenance requirements by facility, system, or component. These approaches require accurate historical data on past maintenance, deterioration trends, and system performance to set repair priorities based on the expected ROI of each repair project. Facility management is also increasingly linked with human resource management through the impact of workplace design and amenities on employee productivity and business results.

CHAPTER SIX

Findings and Recommendations

In this chapter we summarize the findings discussed in the previous chapters and provide our recommendations at the Army, IMCOM, and installation levels.

Findings

Installation Interviews

Based on our site visits and telephone interviews, we heard several consistent themes across locations. First, installation DPWs face staff shortages that can increase facility sustainment costs. For example, DPWs may have to contract out sustainment projects that could be performed less expensively in-house. In some cases, personnel authorizations are capped below TDA requirements, or the TDA was reduced as part of a past public-private competition under Circular A-76. In remote locations, or those outside the continental United States, it can also be difficult to fill vacant positions. Second, the use of GFEBS for real property and facility sustainment has caused a loss of functionality relative to the legacy system. DPW personnel reported that GFEBS is slow and cumbersome to use, it is difficult to get usable management reports, and there is a lack of advanced training and data dictionaries. IMCOM and individual installations have had to develop work-arounds to enter or extract data, such as the DPW Analysis and Reporting Tool. To generate preventive maintenance work orders, DPW personnel must obtain additional training and enter data into GFEBS. At Fort Irwin, the DPW contractor uses Maximo and performs a higher percentage of preventive maintenance work orders than other installations we visited. Finally, DPW staff have benefited from sharing best practices across installations and would like more opportunities to share information with colleagues from other installations.

Each installation used a somewhat different prioritization process for its annual work plan. Fort Detrick uses an IMCOM prioritization matrix based on facility type, project type, ISR rating, and commander's priorities. The highest-priority facility types include firefighting, police, child development centers, Child and Youth Services, barracks, and customer service buildings, such as gyms and Army Community Services buildings. Fort Riley starts with a top-line budget and subtracts "must fund" costs, such as civilian pay and equipment for service orders; support contracts for important services, such as lightning protection, fire alarms, and elevators; and inspections. It then ranks SRM projects into categories based on life/health/safety, prevention of property damage, mission impact, overdue sustainment, and "nice to have." Command emphasis can bring a project to the top of a category but not shift it into a higher-priority category. Fort Irwin also sets aside funding for the DPW facility maintenance contractor and then ranks projects by assigning scores to a long list of factors including life/health/safety, mission impact, compliance with engineering or environmental requirements, resources or energy conservation payback, security or force protection, unit impact or priority, and community interest.

DPW staff at each installation also described practices that they used to allocate funding more efficiently or to improve service. For example, Fort Detrick groups smaller service orders with facility sustainment projects in the same locations to reduce travel time and costs. Fort Riley assigns "estimators" to major tenants to better understand their missions and facilities and help them develop projects for the annual work plan. Several installations have leveraged alternative funding sources for major SRM projects or used community partnerships to reduce the costs of maintaining shared facilities.

Installation Status Report Data Analysis

Installation DPW staff generally agreed that ISR-I ratings reflect the current condition of facilities and can be used to identify specific problem areas. However, it is difficult to examine long-term trends because rating procedures have changed over time. For example, most ISR-I ratings were initially done by tenant building managers, but they are now mostly done by DPW staff or with stronger DPW guidance to improve consistency. In addition, some consolidated assets, such as roads, have been split into separate pieces to better identify problem areas. Some additional concerns are that the ISR-I tends to focus on cosmetic issues, because it is difficult to inspect roofs, foundations, plumbing, and wiring. In some cases, the ratings may not reflect the actual condition of the building unless DPW staff overwrite the estimated repair costs.

Other Services

The Air Force, Navy, and Marine Corps delegate varying amounts of SRM funding to installations. The Air Force has the most centralized process. It delegates about half of SRM funding to installations, and it also uses a central, data-based process to develop installation work plans. The Navy delegates almost all funding to installations but sets detailed priorities for SRM projects. The Marine Corps also delegates most funding to installations, but for the most part allows installations to set their own priorities.

The other services are increasingly using an MDI to prioritize funding based on the importance of the facility and risk of failure to the tenants' mission. The Navy has the most detailed process for assigning MDI ratings based on the mission criticality of facilities. Air Force MDI ratings were initially based on facility CatCodes, but the Air Force is planning to move toward the Navy's process. The other services have also moved faster than the Army in implementing BUILDER and are using tailored facility management software (Maximo and TRIRIGA) to manage maintenance work orders and record maintenance history. In addition, the Air Force uses VAST to make adjustments to the project cost estimates generated by BUILDER.

Facility Management Trends, Practices, and Research

Private-sector organizations tend to focus on minimizing the life-cycle cost of facility ownership. Therefore, functions such as operations and maintenance, SRM, and construction are more integrated to take long-term interactions into account. For example, decisions made during the construction phase affect operations and maintenance costs, and deferred maintenance or sustainment can reduce system life spans and increase replacement costs. Some also use long-range predictive modeling to show the effects of deferred maintenance on life-cycle costs.

Organizations are increasingly linking facility quality and condition with the organizational mission and their effects on employee productivity, absenteeism, and turnover. There are a variety of performance metrics that can be used to evaluate facilities over time and to make comparisons across similar types of buildings, including financial, physical, and functional metrics. The most useful metrics are those that link financial and nonfinancial aspects, are quantifiable and measurable, and are applicable to a wide range of facilities or projects.

Recommendations

Based on our research, we have identified several steps that could be taken to improve the allocation and execution of SRM funding at the Army, IMCOM, and individual installation levels.

Army Level

The Army should consider allowing installations more flexibility on DPW staffing within existing budgets to perform facility sustainment at lower costs. In many cases, installations have to use higher-priced external contractors to design and perform sustainment projects due to DPW staff shortages. In addition, staff shortages affect their ability to enter and analyze data needed to increase emphasis on preventive maintenance and reduce sustainment costs over the long term.

A second important step that the Army could take to better allocate scarce SRM funding is to improve or supplement the real property and facility sustainment functions in GFEBS. IMCOM and the other landholding commands should work with the Office of the Assistant Secretary of the Army for Financial Management and Comptroller in a collaborative manner to improve the real property functions of GFEBS. Actions could include

- creating better training, documentation, and data dictionaries for users
- improving system and network capacity to speed up system performance
- developing better interfaces (or separate systems, such as DART) to enter and extract data and create management reports
- incorporating additional SAP modules to improve real property functions
- allowing cross-communication with BUILDER to update condition assessments and GFEBS's project planning module.

To ensure that user input is incorporated into the process, the Army should consider establishing an IPT or other forum that involves users, the GFEBS contractor, and other stakeholders.

To address the issue of non-fair-wear-and-tear damages in barracks and motor pools, the Army should work to secure authorities to allow costs recovered via Financial Liability Investigations of Property Loss for property damage to be retained at the garrison level to reimburse DPWs for the costs of repairs. This issue also requires Army-level command emphasis to ensure that unit leadership at the company through brigade levels identifies and pursues corrective actions for non-fair-wear-and-tear damages.

Installation Management Command Level

IMCOM should consider creating more opportunities for installation DPW staff to network and share information about common challenges and best practices. These opportunities could include staff visits to other installations to shadow experts, regional conferences, or monthly conference calls on topics of interest.

IMCOM should continue to fund the implementation of BUILDER. During the implementation process, IMCOM, in coordination with the Assistant Chief of Staff for Installation Management, should also determine how ISR-I and BUILDER data will be integrated and used and how ongoing facility condition assessments will be conducted and funded after the initial BUILDER inspections are completed. When BUILDER has been implemented, it can be used to develop longer-range models that show the effects of deferred maintenance on life-cycle costs. In addition, IMCOM should consider developing an MDI that could be used to prioritize projects for the most critical facilities and create linkages between SRM funding and installation readiness. Although these two steps may be costly and difficult in the short run, together they could help justify larger SRM budgets that could eventually reduce the Army's life-cycle costs of facility management.

IMCOM should consider developing a policy memorandum or guidance on identifying alternative sources of funding for SRM projects that are not currently being funded through normal channels as part of the IMCOM Annual Funding Guidance. In an environment of scarce funding, some installations have been able to leverage funding from Army tenant organizations for projects that benefit their mission or from state and local governments for energy and water facility and infrastructure investments. Other installations or tenants may not be aware of these options or have not taken advantage of them, so developing policies or guidance may help increase their use. In addition, these projects can help reduce ongoing sustainment costs and avoid new construction.

IMCOM may also be able to implement some innovative practices from the other services. For example, the Navy is integrating preventive maintenance with updates to BUILDER condition assessments and using BUILDER outputs to consolidate similar projects for economies of scale and to identify high-priority repair and replacement investments over a five-year period. It also conducts midyear evaluations of installations' facility investment strategies. In addition, IMCOM may be able to leverage Navy staff expertise in developing the MDI. The Air Force is making greater use of data and analytical approaches to develop long-range plans and justify funding through the AFCAMP model and IPL. However, given the Army's current data and manpower challenges, these may be longer-term goals.

Installation Level

Installation DPW staff should consider implementing innovative practices that have been successful at other installations. These practices include process improvements, such as grouping routine maintenance work orders by location to increase efficiency or training building tenants or unit representatives to perform minor repair or replacement tasks that do not require a technician, as well as establishing long-term relationships with major tenants to help identify and prioritize sustainment projects.

In addition, installations could increase efforts to identify alternative sources of funding for SRM projects that are not currently being funded through normal channels. Both Army and non-Army tenants may be willing to use mission funding to obtain projects sooner. In some cases, these may be lower-priority projects from the installation's perspective, such as painting or new carpeting, assuming that sufficient DPW manpower is available to perform the work. Installations could also investigate opportunities for reserve component engineering units to perform projects as part of their annual training. Installations should also pursue more IGSAs and other community partnership opportunities to reduce SRM costs.

Additional Installation Status Report Data Analysis

In this appendix we provide additional information on our ISR data analysis. Table A.1 gives some examples of how the Army groups facilities into FCGs, subcategories, categories, and facility classes. The facility class, shown in the first column, is the highest-level aggregation. Each facility class typically consists of several categories (shown in the second column). For the categories shown in bold, we provide a list of subcategories in the third column. Similarly, the fourth column lists the FCGs within the subcategories shown in bold. ISR rolls up facility condition and mission ratings at the FCG, subcategory, category, and facility class levels to provide more aggregated pictures of various types of facility at each installation. In contrast, readiness ratings are only assigned at the facility class level.

Tables A.2 and A.3 show some summary data on facility condition ratings and average transition rates from green or amber to red or black and from red or black to green or amber at each IMCOM-managed installation over the period FY 2010–FY 2017. Table A.2 lists installations with an Army civilian DPW facility sustainment workforce, and Table A.3 lists those with a contractor sustainment workforce. Although there is considerable variation in average facility condition ratings and average transition rates across installations, we did not find any statistically significant differences in the average values for installation DPWs with government civilian workforces versus those with contractor workforces. The bottom line of each table provides a weighted average based on the number of facilities at each installation, which is more directly comparable with the average condition ratings and transition rates shown in Figure 3.6 in Chapter Three. In comparison with the unweighted average ratings, these values suggest that installations with a smaller number of facilities have a smaller percentage rated green and larger percentages rated red or black.

As noted in Chapter Three, the percentage of facilities rated green or amber that transition to red or black is not directly comparable to the percentage of facilities rated red or black that transition to green or amber, because there are typically many more facilities rated green or amber than those rated red or black. Therefore, in the last two columns, we calculate these transition rates as a percentage of all facilities to create more easily comparable transition rates. If the percentage of facilities that is degrading is larger than the percentage that is improving, it suggests that the overall condition of facilities on an installation has been declining over time.

Table A.4 compares FY 2010–FY 2017 average facility condition ratings and transition rates for facilities rated by inspection (as shown in Figure 3.6 in Chapter Three) with those rated by business rule and with the overall average for all facilities. Facilities rated by business rule include generic assets (flagpoles, sidewalks, fire hydrants, traffic signals, and signs); assets that cannot be inspected by direct observation (underground tanks and utilities); those with

Table A.1
Examples of Facility Classifications

Facility Class	Category	Subcategory	FCG
Operations and training	Administrative facilities (operations and training) Information management **Training ranges and areas** Training/instruction facilities	Live fire ranges Maneuver training land **Non-live-fire training facilities**	Confidence/obstacle course Firefighting and rescue Observer tower/bunker Bayonet/assault course
Mobility	Airfield facilities Airfield pavements Deployment facilities Ports Railroads **Road and trail network (mobility)**	Miscellaneous improvements and roads (mobility) Parking—organizational **Surfaced roads**	Surfaced roads Training area roads-surfaced Training area tank trails-surfaced Training area bridges Vehicle bridges
Maintenance and production	**Maintenance facilities** Production facilities	**Maintenance facilities**	Ammunition repair-installation Installation maintenance/repair Vehicle maintenance shops
Research, development, testing, and evaluation	**Research and development**	**Research and development buildings** Research and development facilities other than buildings	Medical research labs RDT&E labs RDT&E range buildings
Supply	**Supply and storage facilities**	Ammunition storage facilities Bulk fuel facilities **General supply and storage facilities** Operational fuel facilities	Covered storage Enclosed storage Hazardous material storage Unit storage buildings Vehicle storage
Housing and community	Child development centers Commissary **Community support** Dining facilities Enlisted UPH Family housing Other UPH	Miscellaneous support facilities Outdoor sports and recreation facilities Physical fitness centers Recreation facilities **Service facilities**	Banks Cemetery Drug counseling facilities Fire/rescue facilities Police/MP stations Postal facilities Thrift shops
Medical	**Hospital and medical facilities**	Dental facilities Dispensaries and clinics Medical centers/hospitals **Medical support facilities** Veterinary facilities	Ambulance shelter Medical warehouses Pharmacy
Administrative	**Administrative facilities** Administrative structure	**General purpose administrative facilities** Unit operations buildings (administrative)	Administrative facilities EOC/SCIF facilities
Utilities and grounds improvement	**Electric/gas** Heat/air conditioning Miscellaneous facilities (utility) Road and trail network (utility) Sewer Utility buildings Waste facilities Water	Electric distribution **Electric source** Electric substations Gas distribution	Electrical power source Standby power

SOURCE: ISR-I data; and Office of the Assistant Chief of Staff for Installation Management, Operations Division, 2017.

NOTES: EOC = Emergency Operations Center; MP = Military Police; RDT&E = Research, Development, Test, and Evaluation; SCIF = Sensitive Compartmented Information Facility; UPH = Unaccompanied Personnel Housing.

Table A.2
Facility Condition Ratings for Installations with Government Civilian Directorates of Public Works

Installation	Number of Facilities (FY 2017)	FY 2010–FY 2017 Average Percentage Rated				Transition Rates Based on Initial Rating		Transition Rates as Percentage of All Facilities	
		Green	Amber	Red	Black	Green or Amber to Red or Black (percent)	Red or Black to Green or Amber (percent)	Green or Amber to Red or Black (percent)	Red or Black to Green or Amber (percent)
Aberdeen Proving Ground	1,651	61	18	15	6	7.7	27.2	5.4	8.0
Adelphi Laboratory	112	81	7	10	2	3.4	33.6	2.6	7.8
Camp Casey/Red Cloud	1,013	58	25	15	2	3.6	34.0	3.3	3.2
Camp Humphreys	668	82	13	3	2	1.0	40.5	1.0	2.2
Fort A. P. Hill	558	66	17	12	5	10.4	31.8	7.8	7.9
Fort Bragg	2,991	70	11	10	9	5.2	34.6	4.1	7.4
Fort Buchanan	420	28	20	31	21	16.7	30.4	7.1	17.5
Fort Campbell	1,482	72	14	11	3	4.5	25.4	3.7	4.7
Fort Detrick	401	90	6	3	1	2.3	38.7	2.1	3.6
Fort Drum	1,574	83	9	6	2	1.0	46.0	0.9	4.7
Fort Greely	173	77	14	6	3	2.5	36.4	2.2	4.4
Fort Hood	3,349	77	10	10	3	5.4	26.8	4.2	5.7
Fort Hunter Liggett	792	65	13	15	7	8.4	28.5	6.4	6.7
Fort Jackson	755	56	20	17	7	9.6	32.0	6.1	11.5
Fort Leavenworth	359	65	14	18	3	6.7	31.7	4.8	8.9
Fort Riley	1,634	80	6	9	5	3.8	29.0	2.9	6.8
Joint Base Lewis McChord	2,664	73	12	10	5	5.6	35.5	4.7	5.7
Natick Soldier Systems Center	265	22	14	41	23	21.3	4.5	7.5	2.9
U.S. Military Academy West Point	861	54	13	23	10	11.9	29.7	6.0	14.6
USAG Bavaria	5,222	77	10	10	3	4.2	28.8	3.1	7.5
USAG Benelux	254	81	10	6	3	1.7	49.4	1.5	5.4
USAG Hawaii	1,776	57	14	18	11	14.5	31.0	8.5	12.9
USAG Italy	602	70	10	16	4	7.1	23.2	4.2	9.4
USAG Japan	2,082	74	12	12	2	4.3	26.4	3.6	4.1
USAG Wiesbaden	1,184	69	14	11	6	5.1	24.7	4.3	4.0
USAG Yongsan	1,115	56	31	11	2	5.5	28.3	4.4	5.7
White Sands Missile Range	3,608	64	8	22	6	2.5	30.9	1.9	7.9
Unweighted average		67.1	13.5	13.6	5.7	6.4	30.8	4.2	7.0
Weighted average		69.7	12.4	12.8	5.1	5.5	30.6	4.0	7.0

Table A.3
Facility Condition Ratings for Installations with Contractor Directorates of Public Works

Installation	Number of Facilities (FY 2017)	FY 2010–FY 2017 Average Percentage Rated				Transition Rates Based on Initial Rating		Transition Rates as Percentage of All Facilities	
		Green	Amber	Red	Black	Green or Amber to Red or Black (percent)	Red or Black to Green or Amber (percent)	Green or Amber to Red or Black (percent)	Red or Black to Green or Amber (percent)
Carlisle Barracks	310	83	9	4	4	1.4	37.9	1.2	4.6
Detroit Arsenal	101	71	9	4	16	3.2	32.3	3.0	2.2
Dugway Proving Ground	635	65	20	11	4	6.9	37.8	5.4	8.4
Fort Belvoir	815	40	26	17	17	10.0	20.4	5.7	8.9
Fort Benning	2,051	76	10	9	5	6.2	41.3	5.2	6.8
Fort Bliss	3,215	84	10	4	2	5.8	37.2	5.3	3.4
Fort Carson	1,379	73	16	8	3	4.5	33.9	3.5	7.7
Fort Gordon	753	70	12	11	7	6.8	40.4	6.0	4.9
Fort Hamilton	225	93	3	3	1	3.0	18.3	2.6	2.0
Fort Huachuca	857	61	17	11	11	5.0	24.4	3.3	8.3
Fort Irwin	688	78	11	9	2	3.5	40.0	3.0	5.9
Fort Knox	1,303	65	12	13	10	5.8	27.3	4.2	7.4
Fort Lee	507	86	8	5	1	2.4	43.7	2.1	4.5
Fort Leonard Wood	1,389	66	18	12	4	5.9	41.3	4.4	10.6
Fort McCoy	1,315	84	9	5	2	1.2	34.1	1.1	2.7
Fort Meade	270	36	30	25	9	15.3	34.4	8.7	14.8
Fort Polk	405	43	12	33	12	15.4	41.4	4.8	28.6
Fort Rucker	1,140	51	20	19	10	10.7	29.1	6.2	12.3
Fort Sill	1,111	80	11	6	3	3.5	37.7	3.1	3.9
Fort Stewart	1,696	58	15	18	9	11.6	30.1	5.8	15.0
Joint Base Myer Henderson Hall	1,527	85	7	6	2	3.4	46.5	3.0	5.9
Picatinny Arsenal	622	43	16	25	16	10.2	30.3	5.8	12.9
Presidio of Monterey	188	86	7	5	2	2.6	35.1	2.3	3.0
Redstone Arsenal	2,061	81	10	7	2	3.4	33.7	3.0	4.5
Rock Island Arsenal	204	64	13	18	5	10.3	44.7	6.9	14.9
USAG Kwajalein Atoll	868	51	20	20	9	18.4	26.7	9.3	13.3
USAG Rheinland-Pfalz[a]	3,824	67	15	13	5	8.0	31.6	5.9	8.4
USAG Soto Cano	168	56	4	24	16	40.6	26.7	24.4	10.7
USAG Stuttgart	885	72	11	13	4	4.2	19.5	2.9	6.1
USAG Wainwright	833	71	15	8	6	3.7	34.0	2.9	7.4
Yuma Proving Ground	939	40	28	29	3	14.5	40.3	8.2	17.6
Unweighted average		67.1	13.7	12.7	6.5	8.0	33.9	5.1	8.6
Weighted average		69.4	13.7	11.5	5.4	6.9	34.3	4.8	8.0

[a] Most USAG Rheinland-Pfalz locations have a contractor DPW workforce, except for Baumholder Military Community, which has a government civilian DPW.

Table A.4
Facility Condition Ratings by Rating Method

Installation	Number of Facilities (FY 2017)	FY 2010–FY 2017 Average Percentage Rated				Transition Rates Based on Initial Rating		Transition Rates as Percentage of All Facilities	
		Green	Amber	Red	Black	Green or Amber to Red or Black (percent)	Red or Black to Green or Amber (percent)	Green or Amber to Red or Black (percent)	Red or Black to Green or Amber (percent)
Rated by inspection	70,239	70	13	12	5	5.9	27.4	5.2	5.0
Rated by business rule	95,313	59	10	18	13	2.2	8.4	1.5	2.6
All	165,552	65	12	15	8	4.5	16.7	3.5	3.9

low benefit relative to costs (gates and fences); unimproved assets (unpaved parking areas and roads); and temporary facilities. Mission and quality ratings generated by business rule are based on the age of the facility, as follows:

- F1/Q1 for permanent, semipermanent, or temporary facilities less than five years old
- F2/Q2 for permanent or semipermanent facilities greater than or equal to five years old and less than 15 years old
- F3/Q3 for permanent or semipermanent facilities greater than or equal to 15 years old
- F4/Q4 for temporary facilities five or more years old.

However, these ratings can be overwritten by the ISR manager based on knowledge of the facility, physical examination, feedback from users, work order history, or other reasons. After an entry is overwritten, it will not be updated by the ISR system as age benchmarks are crossed (see Office of the Assistant Chief of Staff for Installation Management, Operations Division, 2017, Section 14).

As one might expect, Table A.4 indicates that facilities rated by business rule were less likely than those rated by inspection to transition from green or amber to red or black, and vice versa. They also tended to have lower quality ratings than facilities rated by inspection.

Bibliography

Adama, Unekwu J., and Kathy Michell, "Potential Effects of Technological Innovations on Facilities Management Practice," in L. Ruddock, H. Van-Dijk, and C. A. M. Houghton, eds., *International Research Conference 2017: Shaping Tomorrow's Built Environment, Conference Proceedings*, Salford, England: University of Salford, September 2017.

AFCEC—*See* Air Force Civil Engineer Center.

AFIMSC—*See* Air Force Installation and Mission Support Center.

Agarwal, Reena, and Sara Karerat, "Workplace Wellness," *FMJ*, January–February 2019, pp. 53–55. As of May 30, 2019:
http://cdn.coverstand.com/30261/558473/734219121a6dc04ac4b2b99722bf251f3f254bec.8.pdf

Air Force Civil Engineer Center, "AFCAMP Basics Webinar," July 31–August 1, 2017.

Air Force Installation and Mission Support Center, "Introduction to Air Force Category Management," briefing, undated.

Army National Guard, *Readiness Center Transformation Master Plan: Final Report to Congress*, Arlington, Va.: Army National Guard, December 19, 2014.

ARNG—*See* Army National Guard.

Bolten, Joseph G., John M. Halliday, and Edward G. Keating, *Understanding and Reducing the Costs of FORSCOM Installations*, Santa Monica, Calif.: RAND Corporation, MR-730-A, 1996. As of October 30, 2018:
https://www.rand.org/pubs/monograph_reports/MR730.html

Brochner, Jan, "Facilities Management and Trends in Business Services Research," in L. Ruddock, H. Van-Dijk, and C. A. M. Houghton, eds., *International Research Conference 2017: Shaping Tomorrow's Built Environment, Conference Proceedings*, Salford, England: University of Salford, September 2017.

Brown, Chloe, Christos Efstratiou, Ilias Leontiadis, Daniele Quercia, Cecilia Mascolo, James Scott, and Peter Key, "The Architecture of Innovation: Tracking Face-to-Face Interactions with UbiComp Technologies," in *UbiComp'14: Proceedings of the 2014 ACM International Joint Conference on Pervasive and Ubiquitous Computing, Seattle, Washington, September 13–17, 2014*, New York: Association for Computing Machinery, 2014.

Charette, Robert P., and Harold E. Marshall, *UNIFORMAT II Elemental Classification for Building Specifications, Cost Estimating, and Cost Analysis*, Washington, D.C.: U.S. Department of Commerce, NISTIR 6389, October 1999. As of August 6, 2019:
https://arc-solutions.org/wp-content/uploads/2012/03/Charette-Marshall-1999-UNIFORMAT-II-Elemental-Classification....pdf

CNIC—*See* Commander, Navy Installations Command.

Commander, Navy Installations Command, "Conditioned Based Maintenance (CBM)," fact sheet, undated a.

———, "Contact Us," webpage, undated b. As of February 1, 2019:
https://www.cnic.navy.mil/contact_us.html

———, "CBM Report Process," briefing charts, November 14, 2017.

———, "Mission Dependency Index," CNIC Instruction 11100.1A, May 29, 2018.

DBB—*See* Defense Business Board.

De Been, Iris, and Marion Beijer, "The Influence of Office Type on Satisfaction and Perceived Productivity Support," *Journal of Facilities Management*, Vol. 12, No. 2, 2014, pp. 142–157.

Defense Business Board, "Best Practices for Real Property Management," PowerPoint briefing, April 21, 2016. As of December 7, 2018:
https://dbb.defense.gov/Portals/35/Documents/Meetings/2016/2016-04/Real%20Property%20Management%20Presentation%20-%20Approved%2021%20APR%202016.pdf

Defense Manpower Data Center, "DoD Personnel, Workforce Reports & Publications," web database, undated. As of August 6, 2019:
https://www.dmdc.osd.mil/appj/dwp/dwp_reports.jsp

Deputy Chief of Naval Operations (Fleet Readiness and Logistics), "Risk-Based Targeted Facilities Investment Strategy," memorandum, Washington, D.C., Ser N4/17U129049, September 27, 2017.

Deputy Under Secretary of Defense (Installations), *Report to Congress: Identification of Requirements to Reduce the Backlog of Maintenance and Repair of Defense Facilities*, Washington, D.C.: U.S. Department of Defense, April 2001.

DOD—*See* U.S. Department of Defense.

Dowle, Matt, and Arun Srinivasan, "Data.Table: Extension of Data.Frame," R package version 1.11.4, 2018. As of February 7, 2019:
https://CRAN.R-project.org/package=data.table

Email communication with the Real Property Reform Management Group, July 19, 2018.

GAO—*See* U.S. Government Accountability Office.

Grussing, Michael N., *Facility Degradation and Prediction Models for Sustainment, Restoration, and Modernization (SRM) Facility Planning*, Champaign, Ill.: Construction Engineering Research Laboratory, US Army Engineer Research and Development Center, ERDC/CERL TR 12-13, September 2012. As of January 12, 2019:
http://acwc.sdp.sirsi.net/client/en_US/default/index.assetbox.assetactionicon.view/1011382/?rm=CONSTRUCTION+E0%7C%7C%7C1%7C%7C%7C1%7C%7C%7Ctrue

Grussing, Michael N., Kelly M. Dilks, and Matthew C. Walters, *Integration of Sustainment Management Systems (SMS) with the Army Installation Status Report for Infrastructure (ISR-I)*, Champaign, Ill.: Construction Engineering Research Laboratory, US Army Engineer Research and Development Center, ERDC/CERL TR-11-38, September 2011. As of November 5, 2018:
http://www.dtic.mil/dtic/tr/fulltext/u2/a552799.pdf

Grussing, Michael N., Steve Gunderson, Mary Canfield, Ed Falconer, Albert Antelman, and Samuel L. Hunter, *Development of the Army Facility Mission Dependency Index for Infrastructure Asset Management*, Champaign, Ill.: Construction Engineering Research Laboratory, US Army Engineer Research and Development Center, ERDC/CERL TR-10-18, September 2010. As of January 10, 2019:
https://apps.dtic.mil/dtic/tr/fulltext/u2/a552791.pdf

Grussing, Michael N., Donald R. Uzarski, and Lance R. Marrano, "Optimizing Facility Component Maintenance, Repair, and Restoration Investment Strategies Using Financial ROI Metrics and Consequence Analysis," paper presented at the Ninth International Conference on Applications of Advanced Technology in Transportation, Chicago, August 13–16, 2006.

Headquarters, U.S. Department of the Army, "Installation Status Report Program," Army Regulation 210-14, August 7, 2012. As of November 5, 2018:
https://www.imcomacademy.com/ima/wp-content/uploads/2013/06/AR_210-14_rev_7Aug12.pdf

Horn, Donnie, "Intro to the Execution Plan: 'Ex Plan 101,'" Air Force Installation and Mission Support Command, briefing, March 26, 2018.

IBM Corporation, "Understanding the Impact and Value of Enterprise Asset Management," white paper, 2016. As of January 12, 2019:
https://www-01.ibm.com/common/ssi/cgi-bin/ssialias?htmlfid=tib14016usen

Interview with Fort Hood DPW personnel, May 3, 2019.

Keating, Edward G., Dina G. Levy, Joy S. Moini, Susan M. Gates, Kristin Leuschner, Candice Riley, Tessa Kaganoff, and Catherine H. Augustine, *The Effects of A-76 Cost Comparisons on DoD Civilian Education and Training*, Santa Monica, Calif.: RAND Corporation, DB-442-OSD, 2006. As of October 30, 2018: https://www.rand.org/pubs/documented_briefings/DB442.html

Koo, Wei Lin, "Thinking Like a CFO: Prevention Pays, Analysis Shows," FacilitiesNet, December 1, 2002. As of January 21, 2019: https://www.facilitiesnet.com/maintenanceoperations/article/Thinking-Like-a-CFO-Prevention-Pays -Analysis-Shows--1505

Koo, Wei Lin, and Tracy Van Hoy, "Determining the Economic Value of Preventive Maintenance," white paper, Chicago: Jones Lang LaSalle, undated.

Kuhr, Greg, and David Carr, "Pre-Command Garrison Leaders Course: HQ IMCOM G4, Facilities and Logistics," PowerPoint briefing, October 2017.

Lachman, Beth E., Jaime L. Hastings, Mary Kate Adgie, Bradley M. Knopp, and Steven Deane-Shinbrot, *Improving Army Installation Facility Sharing and Land-Use Deals and Partnerships*, Santa Monica, Calif.: RAND Corporation, RR-2696-A, 2019. As of September 12, 2019: https://www.rand.org/pubs/research_reports/RR2696.html

Lachman, Beth E., Ellen M. Pint, Aimee E. Curtright, and Cole Sutera, *Alternatives for Reducing Army Installation Utility Bills While Enhancing Installation Readiness*, Santa Monica, Calif.: RAND Corporation, RR-2773-1-A, forthcoming.

Lachman, Beth E., Susan A. Resetar, and Frank Camm, *Military Installation Public-to-Public Partnerships: Lessons from Past and Current Experiences*, Santa Monica, Calif.: RAND Corporation, RR-1419-A/AF/NAVY/OSD, 2016. As of October 5, 2018: https://www.rand.org/pubs/research_reports/RR1419.html

Lachman, Beth E., Susan A. Resetar, Nidhi Kalra, Agnes Gereben Schaefer, and Aimee E. Curtright, *Water Management, Partnerships, Rights, and Market Trends: An Overview for Army Installation Managers*, Santa Monica, Calif.: RAND Corporation, RR-933-A, 2016. As of October 5, 2018: https://www.rand.org/pubs/research_reports/RR933.html

Lavy, Sarel, and Manish K. Dixit, "Key Performance Indicators for Facility Performance Assessment: Measuring Core Indicators Using Building Information Modeling," in L. Ruddock, H. Van-Dijk, and C. A. M. Houghton, eds., *International Research Conference 2017: Shaping Tomorrow's Built Environment, Conference Proceedings*, Salford, England: University of Salford, September 2017.

Lavy, Sarel, John A. Garcia, and Manish K. Dixit, "Establishment of KPIs for Facility Performance Measurement: Review of Literature," *Facilities*, Vol. 28, Nos. 9–10, 2010, pp. 440–464.

———, "KPIs for Facility's Performance Assessment, Part I: Identification and Categorization of Core Indicators," *Facilities*, Vol. 32, Nos. 5–6, 2014a, pp. 256–274.

———, "KPIs for Facility's Performance Assessment, Part II: Identification of Variables and Deriving Expressions for Core Indicators," *Facilities*, Vol. 32, Nos. 5–6, 2014b, pp. 275–294.

Lavy, Sarel, John A. Garcia, Phil Scinto, and Manish K. Dixit, "Key Performance Indicators for Facility Performance Assessment: Simulation of Core Indicators," *Construction Management and Economics*, Vol. 32, No. 12, 2014, pp. 1183–1204.

Lewis, Bernard T., and Richard Payant, *Facility Manager's Maintenance Handbook*, 2nd ed., New York: The McGraw-Hill Companies, Inc., 2007.

Life Cycle Engineering Inc., "Analyzing the Relationship of Preventive Maintenance to Corrective Maintenance," undated. As of April 3, 2019: https://www.lce.com/Analyzing-the-Relationship-of-Preventive-Maintenance-to-Corrective-Maintenance -1091.html

Lister, Kate, "Show Me the Money: The Bottom Line on Workplace Change," *FMJ*, January–February 2019, pp. 38–42. As of May 30, 2019: http://cdn.coverstand.com/30261/558473/734219121a6dc04ac4b2b99722bf251f3f254bec.8.pdf

Little, Vince, "DOIM Takes New Name but 'Mission Has Not Changed,'" *The Bayonet*, September 29, 2009. As of May 10, 2019:
https://www.army.mil/article/27982/doim_takes_new_name_but_mission_has_not_changed

Maglio, Paul P., and Chie-Hyeon Lim, "Innovation and Big Data in Smart Service Systems," *Journal of Innovation Management*, Vol. 4, No. 1, 2016, pp. 11–21.

Maguire, Ed, and John Hurd, "Stretching Sustainment Dollars: Realizing Value Through Facility Condition Assessments," *The Military Engineer*, Vol. 107, No. 697, 2015. As of July 19, 2018:
http://themilitaryengineer.com/index.php/tme-articles/tme-magazine-online/item/501-stretching-sustainment-dollars-realizing-value-through-facility-condition-assessments

Martin, Casey, and Laverne Deckert, "ISO 41000: Improving Overall Facility Performance," *FMJ*, January–February 2019, pp. 21–23. As of May 30, 2019:
http://cdn.coverstand.com/30261/558473/734219121a6dc04ac4b2b99722bf251f3f254bec.8.pdf

MyBaseGuide, "Fort Irwin Units," webpage, October 15, 2015. As of October 26, 2018:
http://www.mybaseguide.com/army/51-210/fort_irwin_irwin_units

———, "Fort Riley 2017–2018 Guide and Directory," 2017. As of October 26, 2018:
http://www.mybaseguide.com/Military-Relocation-Guide/627/Fort Riley

National Center for Education Statistics, *Postsecondary Education Facilities Inventory and Classification Manual*, 2006 ed., Washington, D.C.: National Center for Education Statistics, 2006. As of June 27, 2018:
https://nces.ed.gov/pubs2006/ficm/toc.asp

National Research Council, *Budgeting for Facilities Maintenance and Repair Activities*, Washington, D.C.: National Academies Press, Report Number 131, 1996. As of August 5, 2019:
https://www.nap.edu/catalog/9226/budgeting-for-facilities-maintenance-and-repair-activities-report-number-131

Office of Management and Budget, "Performance of Commercial Activities," Circular No. A-76 (Revised), May 29, 2003. As of October 30, 2018:
https://www.whitehouse.gov/sites/whitehouse.gov/files/omb/circulars/A76/a76_incl_tech_correction.pdf

Office of the Assistant Chief of Staff for Installation Management, *Real Property Summary Installation and Site Statistics for Fiscal Year 2017 Quarter 4*, Washington, D.C.: Department of the Army, March 15, 2017.

Office of the Assistant Chief of Staff for Installation Management, Operations Division, *FY18 ISR Infrastructure Implementing Instructions*, Version 1.0, Washington, D.C.: Department of the Army, October 1, 2017.

Office of the Assistant Secretary of Defense for Sustainment, Facilities Investment and Management, "FIM Program Areas," webpage, undated. As of November 15, 2018:
https://www.acq.osd.mil/eie/fim/FIM_Program_Areas.html

Office of the Chief Management Officer, "Real Property Management Reform—Portfolio Prioritization and Optimization," memorandum, Washington, D.C., June 5, 2018.

R Core Team, *R: A Language and Environment for Statistical Computing*, Vienna: R Foundation for Statistical Computing, Vienna, Austria, 2018. As of June 19, 2019:
https://www.R-project.org/

RSMeans Data, homepage, undated. As of August 6, 2019:
https://www.rsmeans.com/products/online.aspx

RStudio Team, *RStudio: Integrated Development for R*, Boston: RStudio Inc., 2016. As of June 19, 2019:
http://www.rstudio.com/

Sailer, Kerstin, Ros Pomeroy, and Rosie Haslem, "Data-Driven Design: Using Data on Human Behaviour and Spatial Configuration to Inform Better Workplace Design," *Corporate Real Estate Journal*, Vol. 4, No. 3, 2015, pp. 249–262.

SchoolDude, *An Ounce of Prevention Is Worth a Pound of Cure: Examining the Costs, Benefits and Best Practices of a Preventive Maintenance Plan in Your Educational Institution*, Cary, N.C.: Dude Solutions, 2013. As of December 20, 2018:
http://explore.schooldude.com/rs/schooldude/images/Preventive%20Maintenance%20Whitepaper.pdf

Smith, Michael, "1st Cavalry Division's Tactical Vehicle Wash Facility Re-Opens," *Fort Hood Sentinel*, June 14, 2018. As of June 16, 2019:
http://www.forthoodsentinel.com/news/st-cavalry-divison-s-tactical-vehicle-wash-facility-re-opens/article_d11accb0-6f15-11e8-9b07-f3851efc8c98.html

Swanson, Laura, "Linking Maintenance Strategies to Performance," *International Journal of Production Economics*, Vol. 70, No. 3, April 2001, pp. 237–244.

Thompson, Tom, Kurt Sorensen, and Melinda Buckrop, "Life Cycle Analysis of a Life Cycle Management System," paper presented at the SAME-IFMA Facilities Management Workshop, San Antonio, Tex., February 7–9, 2018.

Thompson Gray Inc., "Corporate Capabilities," March 2018. As of August 14, 2019:
https://thompsongrayinc.com/pdf/Thompson-Gray-Capabilities-Mar-2018.pdf

Under Secretary of Defense for Acquisition, Technology and Logistics, "Standardizing Facility Condition Assessments," memorandum, Washington, D.C., September 10, 2013. As of January 12, 2019:
https://www.acq.osd.mil/eie/Downloads/FIM/DoD%20Facility%20Inspection%20Policy.pdf

Under Secretary of Defense (Comptroller), *Construction Programs (C-1)*, FY 2007–FY 2019, 2006–2018a. As of December 6, 2018:
https://comptroller.defense.gov/Budget-Materials/

———, *Operation and Maintenance Overview*, FY 2007–FY 2019, 2006–2018b. As of December 6, 2018:
https://comptroller.defense.gov/Budget-Materials/

———, *Defense Budget Overview: United States Department of Defense Fiscal Year 2019 Budget Request*, February 13, 2018. As of December 6, 2018:
https://comptroller.defense.gov/Portals/45/Documents/defbudget/fy2019/FY2019_Budget_Request_Overview_Book.pdf

U.S. Army, Fort Detrick, *Fort Detrick Welcome Guide 2016–2017*, undated. As of October 25, 2018:
https://www.dcmilitary.com/base_guides/fort_detrick/eedition/page/page_206977e0-e36a-5d5b-a8c0-f89c0979179d.html

U.S. Army, Fort Irwin, "Installation Fact Sheet," 2017.

U.S. Army, Fort Riley, "1st Infantry Division," webpage, undated a. As of August 5, 2019:
https://home.army.mil/riley/index.php/tenants/1st-ID

———, "Garrison Partners," webpage, undated b. As of August 5, 2019:
https://home.army.mil/riley/index.php/tenants/partners

U.S. Army Garrison Rheinland-Pfalz, "History," webpage, undated a. As of October 26, 2018:
https://home.army.mil/rheinland-pfalz/index.php/about/history

———, "My USAG RP," webpage, undated b. As of October 26, 2018:
https://home.army.mil/rheinland-pfalz/index.php/usag-rheinland-pfalz

———, "Units/Tenants," webpage, undated c. As of August 5, 2019:
https://home.army.mil/rheinland-pfalz/index.php/units-tenants

U.S. Department of the Army, *Fiscal Year (FY) 2019 Budget Estimates: Operation and Maintenance, Army, Volume I*, February 2018. As of August 5, 2019:
https://www.asafm.army.mil/Portals/72/Documents/BudgetMaterial/2019/Base%20Budget/Operation%20and%20Maintenance/Army%20-%20Vol%201%20Justification%20Book.pdf

U.S. Department of Defense, *Base Structure Report—Fiscal Year 2017 Baseline*, September 30, 2016. As of March 26, 2019:
https://www.acq.osd.mil/eie/Downloads/BSI/Base%20Structure%20Report%20FY17.pdf

———, *Unified Facilities Criteria (UFC): DoD Facilities Pricing Guide*, UFC 3-701-01, Change 1, June 25, 2018. As of August 16, 2019:
https://www.wbdg.org/ffc/dod/unified-facilities-criteria-ufc/ufc-3-701-01

U.S. Department of Defense, Office of the Inspector General, *Army Needs to Improve Controls and Audit Trails for the General Fund Enterprise Business System Acquire-to-Retire Business Process*, Washington, D.C.: U.S. Department of Defense, Office of Inspector General, Report No. DODIG-2013-130, September 13, 2013. As of October 31, 2018:
https://media.defense.gov/2013/Sep/13/2001713303/-1/-1/1/DODIG-2013-130.pdf

U.S. General Services Administration, "FY 2016 Federal Real Property Profile (FRPP) Open Data Set," spreadsheet, September 30, 2016. As of August 27, 2018:
https://www.gsa.gov/cdnstatic/FY_2016_Open_Data_Set.xlsx

U.S. Government Accountability Office, *Defense Facility Condition: Revised Guidance Needed to Improve Oversight of Assessments and Ratings*, Washington, D.C.: U.S. Government Accountability Office, GAO-16-662, June 2016. As of November 15, 2018:
https://www.gao.gov/assets/680/677972.pdf

Uzarski, Donald R., Michael N. Grussing, and James B. Clayton, "Knowledge-Based Condition Survey Inspection Concepts," *ASCE Journal of Infrastructure Systems*, Vol. 13, No. 1, March 2007, pp. 72–79.

Van der Voordt, Theo J. M., "Productivity and Employee Satisfaction in Flexible Workplaces," *Journal of Corporate Real Estate*, Vol. 6, No. 2, 2004, pp. 133–148.

Walker, Alexander, "openxlsx: Read, Write and Edit XLSX Files," R package version 4.1.0, 2018. As of February 7, 2019:
https://CRAN.R-project.org/package=openxlsx

Weitzel, Mikhael, "History of Army Contracting," April 4, 2011. As of May 10, 2019:
https://www.army.mil/article/54337/history_of_army_contracting

Wendl, Joseph, "Incorporating Asset Management into the Sustainability Mission," unpublished manuscript, shared with the authors, Fort Bragg, N.C., December 2018.

Wickham, Hadley, and Jennifer Bryan, "readxl: Read Excel Files," R package version 1.1.0, 2018. As of February 7, 2019:
https://CRAN.R-project.org/package=readxl

Willman, Alexander J., "Preparing for the Future: Owning Your O&M Budget," *FMJ*, March-April 2019, pp. 30–33. As of May 30, 2019:
http://cdn.coverstand.com/30261/572553/59d6775e388a028f470d5bb58c762cf6b8cd2fa1.35.pdf